THE HARD WAY
AN MBA

AN MBA
THE HARD WAY
FAITH, FAMILY, OIL FIELDS, AND GOLF

Lynn & Jack,
Hope you enjoy the read!

Dave

DAVE HENTSCHEL

TATE PUBLISHING
AND ENTERPRISES, LLC

An MBA the Hard Way
Copyright © 2013 by Dave Hentschel. All rights reserved.

No part of this publication may be reproduced, stored in a retrieval system or transmitted in any way by any means, electronic, mechanical, photocopy, recording or otherwise without the prior permission of the author except as provided by USA copyright law.

Scripture quotations, unless otherwise indicated, are taken from the Holy Bible, King James Version, Cambridge, 1769. Used by permission. All rights reserved.

Scripture quotations marked (NKJV) are taken from the New King James Version. Copyright © 1982 by Thomas Nelson, Inc. Used by permission. All rights reserved.

The opinions expressed by the author are not necessarily those of Tate Publishing, LLC.

Published by Tate Publishing & Enterprises, LLC
127 E. Trade Center Terrace | Mustang, Oklahoma 73064 USA
1.888.361.9473 | www.tatepublishing.com

Tate Publishing is committed to excellence in the publishing industry. The company reflects the philosophy established by the founders, based on Psalm 68:11,
"The Lord gave the word and great was the company of those who published it."

Book design copyright © 2013 by Tate Publishing, LLC. All rights reserved.
Cover design by Ronnel Luspoc
Interior design by Honeylette Pino

Published in the United States of America

ISBN: 978-1-62295-540-4
1. Biography & Autobiography / Personal Memoirs
2. Biography & Autobiography / Business
13.06.18

DEDICATION

It will be apparent as you read this book that the whole story is dedicated to the people who are the heart of the story. To Clydella; to Scott, Erin, Emily, and Lindsey; to Stuart, Cathy, Annie, and Ella; and to Steve and Debbie, who I think of every day. And to all the people that made me much better than I would have been on my own. Also, as will be evident in the reading, to my God, who I love with all my heart.

On June 19, 2012, the very special lady with whom I shared all the events of the book passed away. Clydella, my wife of 53 years, whose efforts while the kids were growing up allowed me to participate in the events related in the book, went to be with the Lord. Clydella, whose efforts after the boys were grown, were directed to helping others through her participation in almost twenty not-for-profit agencies over the last thirty-five years. Her last year was not a good one. She knew over the last eight months what the outcome was going to be. In the end, she was ready to spend eternity with Christ. She is missed by family and friends, but most of all by me.

ACKNOWLEDGMENTS

I thank God for Clydella and all that she means to me; for Scott and Erin; Stephen and Debbie; Stuart and Cathy; and Emily, Lindsey, Annie, and Ella; for friends that we have been blessed to know; for a special church and Sunday school class that are the source of so many blessings; for the special people that I was allowed to work with and meant so much to me, especially Dale; and for the very special country where I was born and allowed to live all my life.

I also would like to thank Tom Winters and Elizabeth Sherman for all their assistance with the book.

CONTENTS

Preface 11
A Family on the Move 15
Boone Pickens A-01 41
    Lesson 1: Hello, Corporate Raiders 41
    Lesson 2: Expect the Unexpected 44
    Lesson 3: Relationships Matter 49
    Lesson 4: Don't Be Naïve 51
    Lesson 5: God Is Just 57
Going Upstream 61
Expansion of Mind and Heart 87
The End of an Era 113
Changing Direction 131
The Canadian Adventure 149
At Last…Bakersfield 173
New Adventures 185
An Old Oilman's Perspective 199
Summing Up My MBA 217
    1. God Is Interested 217
    2. People Are More Important than Things 219
    3. The Bible Has the Answers 221
    4. You Are Blessed to Be a Blessing 224
    5. No Matter What Happens, God Is There 227

PREFACE

Over a year ago, I sat down to write about some events in my life that I believed were significant, at least to me. I felt I had been privileged to be a part of those events, but I regretted that they often took me away from my growing family. Since I was gone a lot from 1979 to 1999, I thought my grown children, and even my wife, should have some idea what I was up to during that period of their lives. I wanted them to know why I traveled while other fathers were at home most of the time, and why we moved around the country almost every three years.

As I progressed into the writing, it seemed this would be more of a business book because the events I was a part of were significant from that standpoint. Not only were the circumstances special, but also the people involved were even more so. It struck me that there were no early signs in my life or career that I would be privileged to be a part of events such as these. As I continued to write however, I realized my experience had much more to do with a commitment I had made to God during those years than any abilities or expertise I displayed as I moved from job to job.

I began to feel like the colt that carried Jesus on his back on Palm Sunday. During the procession, that young donkey probably thought, *Wow, these people really think I'm something!* It was only afterward that he realized the people weren't looking at him: they were looking at the One he carried. The more I wrote, the more I realized this wasn't really a book about business transactions that changed our world, but about a relationship with Jesus Christ that changed me and thus had some effect on the world in which I lived. It became apparent to me that any significant thing about me has always had to do with my relationship with Him.

I have been asked what it is that I want the reader to take away from this book. What wisdom do I want to impart? I am not sure I have thought about anything that profound during the writing! However, I do know what is obvious to me after relating this account of my life: through all the crises and triumphs, turmoil and joy, and every decision that brought either calamity or success, underneath it all was my ever-faithful Lord and Savior. He was there, patiently leading me and guiding me, humbling me when I was tempted to take credit, and comforting me when life threw Clydella and me some terrible curveballs. He was there then, he is here now, and will always be there and that's why I know the future is bright and not to be feared.

My journey with Jesus set me on the path for obtaining an MBA, not only in business, but also in life. It certainly wasn't my good looks, charm, or intelligence, although my wife might say that was part of it! My success in business and family life, the many friends I have been blessed with along the way, even the tremendous fun I have had along the way, are all a result of His amazing grace. And you should know right now that He and I are still working on it. This MBA degree isn't completed yet!

As you read this book, I hope you will see even more than I have that Jesus told the truth when he said, "With God, all things are possible." If anyone's life illustrates that statement, it is mine.

A FAMILY ON THE MOVE

When you look back on your life, you see how extraordinary so many times were, times you never considered extraordinary while you were living them. By extraordinary, I don't necessarily mean fame, fortune, or tremendous achievements. I'm talking about times that made you the person you are now. As you return to the past and examine the little details of your life, all those little details become significant, even precious. You find they not only connected you intimately to the people who loved you, influenced you, and helped to mold your character, but also you see the hand of God in them. And that is something that fills you with awe. He not only cared, he gave your life meaning and purpose.

It was a long time before I began to see any of this, a long time before I really allowed my Creator to get involved in my life and do some pretty creative things. Even after that commitment was made and I understood clearly what I believed, there was always that problem of living my life in a way that reflected those beliefs. My daily life often includes thoughts and actions that conflict with my beliefs! There is also the connection from your heart to your brain that must be in sync as you lead your life, and that is very difficult.

But our God is in the business of forgiveness because He knows the world in which we live.

Growing up, my life seemed so ordinary. I was born on February 12, 1934, in Kansas City, Kansas. I think I lived there all of nine months. By the time we arrived in Shreveport, Louisiana, when I was three-and-a-half, we had moved several times. My dad was a salesman of oil field equipment. He was also probably the best equipment repairman in the Arkansas-Louisiana-Texas region, and I was proud of him.

By 1937, my dad's job kept him out of town close to four days out of seven. For that reason my mother, Laura, was responsible for raising the family. I'm proud of her too. We were never wealthy, but we were hardly ever in need. My brother was six years older than I, and that, in addition to the fact that we had completely different interests, led to us never being very close. My sister and I are much closer. That's just the way it turned out.

Sports were my passion, and I grew up playing football, basketball, and baseball. I was probably average in all those sports, but I was a good teammate, always giving everything I had to the teams I played with. I started playing baseball when I was in the third grade. Later, I would play on an American Legion team where at least seven or eight of us had been playing together since the third grade. It was also helpful that one of those guys was a left-handed pitcher who, upon high school graduation in 1952, signed a major league contract that included a $50,000 bonus. We were always grateful that we never had to hit against him!

My mom and dad were like most parents during the late thirties and forties, very conservative and very strict. Since Dad was gone most of the time, Mom saw to it that we were at the Highland Baptist Church every Sunday. I spent a lot of time in church, either mine or at the churches my friends attended. During the summer, we would go to a variety of vacation Bible schools when we were younger, and youth meetings when we got older, to occupy the times we were not playing baseball or some other sport. There is no question that the church was the center of our lives, whether in school or out of school.

When I was twelve years old, I gave my life to Jesus and was baptized. There was never any doubt in my mind that what I did was real. I knew I had sinned. I knew I couldn't save myself. And I knew Jesus died for my sins so that God could forgive me. When I received Jesus as my Lord and Savior, I immediately knew deep inside that I was okay with God and would go to heaven when I died. I was truly a Christian, even though I probably could not explain fully what it meant when I said that. Although it would be some time before I committed to *living* in accordance with what I knew and said I was, God's Holy Spirit was always inside me, nudging me to do the right thing. I wish I could say that I always listened!

I worked many jobs to have spending money that was not otherwise available. I had an early morning paper route for a couple of years. I sold *Liberty* magazines house to house. I delivered milk off a truck on Saturdays. When I got older, I worked at an Esso filling station all day on Saturdays. That was when gas stations employed attendants to fill your tank, check your oil, check your tire pressure, and wipe your windshield. During Christmas break one year, I worked at the National Shirt Shop.

My graduating class from Byrd High School was very special. As of this writing, we are coming up on our sixtieth anniversary and still have many members of the class attend anytime we have a reunion. I have one very close friend with whom I went from the first grade through college, and we continue to talk at least every month. Since I have not lived in Louisiana since 1961, I have lost touch with many people of whom I have very fond memories.

There is one extraordinary thing about my early life: nothing during that time lingers as a bad memory. I had challenges and obstacles to overcome, but all of my memories of growing up are good.

* * *

It was a big deal for me to go to college, and I went to a good one. In September of 1952, I entered Louisiana State University (LSU) and majored in petroleum engineering. The first year was spent studying, and I had a good scholastic record to show for it. That year I spent much of my free time at the Baptist Student Union and participated in many of their activities. I think it was during that year that a very young Billy Graham had a crusade in Baton Rouge. I got a chance to meet him during the event. I am sure neither he nor

I had any idea how the Lord would use him throughout the world during his long and very active ministry.

In my second year at LSU, I joined a fraternity, Kappa Sigma, and my commitment changed from academics to having a good time. The rest of my college career was a whole lot of fun, but school requirements too often interfered with my social life. I was always able to talk myself through sticky situations, and I came to believe that gift would get me through anything I encountered in life.

During college breaks, I worked as a laborer on a domestic pipeline company, replacing old lines, cutting right-of-way and any other thing I was told to do.[1] I think the going rate during those years was $1.04 per hour. It didn't amount to much, but it sure passed the time of day until school started again. While I eventually graduated, I have never been happy with my performance during the last years. If I could do it all over again, however, I probably wouldn't change a thing!

I spent four years in the Air Force ROTC while at LSU, and in June of 1957, I reported to Lackland Air Force Base with a commitment to become a pilot. At that time, the Air Force was flooded with pilots and wannabe pilots. I flunked my flight physical because of some unknown ear problem, which has never surfaced since then. They promptly sent me to an airman first class to decide what I would do to fulfill my commitment of three years.

The first question the airman first class asked me was, "What's your degree in?"

"Petroleum engineering."

Without hesitation, he said, "I think we'll make a weatherman out of you."

I replied, "I don't understand the connection, but tell me about it."

"The Air Force will send you back to school for a year to study meteorology."

I asked the obvious. "What is my connection to the Air Force during this year?"

"We'll send you a check every month, and you don't have to wear a uniform."

"Sir, you have found exactly what I want to be. Where do I go to school?"

"You have a choice," and he handed me a list of schools. It didn't take me long to ask for Florida State. "Sorry, you're too late. The class is full." I next said Stanford. "If you are looking for something on the coast, they are already filled."

As I searched the list, I thought of some people I knew in Oklahoma. "How about Oklahoma State?"

He said, "No problem," and a few days later, I was on the campus of OSU, living in a second-story apartment with some other guys who were Kappa Sigs. I affiliated with my fraternity when I got to Stillwater mainly so I could eat there for about forty dollars a month, which was about all I had left after paying my bills.

About two weeks into school, I went on a double date. That was when I met Clydella, who was out with the other guy. We actually double-dated a couple of times, each seeing other people, but I couldn't help but notice her good looks and great personality. She appeared to be more transparent and down-to-earth than the other girls I was seeing. From the very first time we met, I think we both knew we would get together.

After almost a month, I asked her out, and we went out thirty-nine nights in a row! I learned she had one older sister and her father was the superintendent of schools in Guymon, Oklahoma, and her mother, a teacher in that system. Her dad was also a huge sports fan, and Clydella was his sports partner. They drove all over Oklahoma and Texas to watch games. The first time Clydella took me to visit her family, we went to Kansas City to see the Yankees play baseball. I knew this was the girl for me! Throughout our marriage, we have enjoyed sports of all kinds, although I enjoy golf more than she does. Of course, OSU basketball is at the top of the list, where we have had season tickets for the last twenty-two years.

When I met her, Clydella was a senior at OSU, majoring in elementary education. During Christmas break, she got a call from her school counselor who indicated there was an opening for a teacher in Ponca City, Oklahoma. If she took that job, she would not have to come back and take finals. Needless to say, she took it. I always wondered if there was anything I wouldn't do if someone made me the same offer. So the next semester, one of us was driving back and forth from Ponca City to Stillwater every week.

We got engaged in July of 1958. The classes I was taking in meteorology would be completed the end of September, and I knew I would have my orders by then, so we got married in Clydella's home town of Guymon on September 6, 1958. Everything went according to plan except for the night of the rehearsal. There was a fight her dad and I wanted to see, a middleweight championship bout between Tony Demarco and Carmen Basilio, so her dad informed the minister that our time was limited. The minister hurried, and we did watch the fight that night!

My generation was much less sophisticated than the current generation. Clydella and I probably knew less about each other before our marriage than most people do nowadays, but we made a commitment not many make today either. That commitment went beyond our knowledge of each other or what we believed our lives would be like. To some extent, it involved an understanding that God would see us through because he brought us together, with the help of that airman first class in Texas! Also, we committed to work out any problems in ways that were acceptable to God and to both of us. It has worked well for over fifty years now.

I know that I would not have the family I have, or have been able to accomplish what I have in business or in the communities in which we lived without Clydella. That will become apparent to you as you read on. She is my friend, my wife, the mother of my children, my love, my lover, and my partner in Christ. She has brought joy to my life in a way no one else could.

* * *

By the time of our wedding, I had been given orders to report to Seymour Johnson Air Force Base in Goldsboro, North Carolina, where I would work as a weather forecaster. Clydella got a teaching job there over the phone before the wedding, and we moved to Goldsboro as soon as I finished my classes. Then, after over a year of forecasting weather, I left the Air Force in December 1959, and we returned to Oklahoma.

Two significant things happened to Clydella and me in 1960. In January, I entered an engineering training program as a reservoir engineer with Arkansas Fuel Oil Corporation and began travelling extensively throughout the southwest. By the end of the year, Cities Service Company had acquired the controlling interest of Arkansas Fuel Oil Corporation, and this began my long career with Cities Service. Also, that year, our son Scott was born in Guymon. Clydella will tell you I missed the birth, but I drove all night from Shreveport, Louisiana, to arrive one hour after the birth. This hardly made up for her being alone except for her family during childbirth, but it was just the way it happened.

And so, Clydella and I became parents, and my career began that long climb up the corporate ladder without any idea where it would lead. I commenced on-the-job courses for my MBA in life, and a year later, we moved to Odessa, Texas. I was based there as a production and drilling engineer from 1961 through 1963. It is also where our son Steve was born in 1962. We had very little money, but it didn't seem like a hardship; it was just how it was. It made no difference in my case since I was never home. I was spending all of my time in the field, sleeping in my car, supervising up to six drilling rigs and many other related projects.

In 1964, Cities moved me to Bartlesville, Oklahoma, where I was a gas engineer, but that didn't last long. I had a disagreement with one of the higher-ups in the production division, the department in which I was working, so I accepted a job the following year in the purchasing department as a buyer. Although it didn't make sense to many of my cohorts, it was one of the best moves I ever made.

Stuart was born in 1965, probably as a direct result of me coming back in town for a while after a strike of the labor union that served the oil industry. A bunch of us were sent to do the jobs of people who were not working. Shortly after returning from that assignment, Clydella became pregnant. We were always blessed with no problems becoming pregnant; we just needed the time to be together.

Our life with our kids was pretty typical. One of the things about raising my sons was that there was hardly anything they did that was different than what I had done at their respective ages. In many respects, they were totally predictable. Later, when we had granddaughters, we discovered that almost nothing is predictable with them! There was a drama involved with girls that was not present with our boys, but it was a wonderful difference.

During my sons' early years, I worked to see if we could ever get to the point that we had more money coming in than we had going out, and Clydella helped by substitute teaching. Again, I thank God for her. She often had to be mother and father, and everything else that was required for our three boys, and she is still a great mother. Our children were very normal and involved in everything to do with sports and being boys.

In 1968, I became manager of the motor transportation department at Cities, which eventually moved us to Tulsa, Oklahoma, in 1969. I was responsible for the rolling stock of the company and the garages that serviced them, along with all the operating machinery in the production division of the company. Friends and family asked how a petroleum engineer ended up in motor transportation. I had no idea then, but God did! I can look back and understand how each promotion was a meaningful stepping-stone to where I finally ended up at Cities.

In 1970, our family had to make a difficult move. At that time, the corporate offices of Cities Service were in New York City, and I was being considered for a new position in that office. The challenge was to bring fifteen separate purchasing offices throughout North America under one organization. The majority of people being considered for the position had more experience than I had, and I realized it was a long shot. By this time in my career, I was very much aware of the maneuvering that takes place inside a large corporation, and I knew just enough to know it wasn't something I was fond of.

As I said earlier, I had given my life to Jesus Christ at a young age, but I never thought my business life was part of that commitment. Actually, I wasn't sure whether God wanted to deal with my professional life. As I was cooling down from a run one evening, I decided to see if God had an interest in my career. I prayed a very specific prayer: "God, if you would take over my business life, I will listen and go and do whatever you have in mind." I was completely in earnest.

I am not sure what I thought would happen after praying such a prayer, but what is clear in my mind now is that if God had chosen a different path for Clydella and me, we would have been satisfied regardless of what that might have been. The truth is that the path he chose was not even in our wildest dreams and certainly not in the range of what I considered my own abilities.

※ ※ ※

Fantastic as it seemed, I got the job as general manager of purchasing in New York City. I was one of about ten guys who were transferred there at the same time. Until our families got there after school was out, we all lived in midtown Manhattan at the Ambassador Hotel. Our offices were in Downtown New York City. In our three-month stay, we learned more about the streets of New York than we ever wanted to know. We would finish work, get on the subway, and then walk about three blocks from the subway to the hotel. New York City was a different place in the early 1970s. There were prostitutes almost all the way to the hotel, and we ran that gauntlet every day.

One of the first evenings we were there, seven of us ventured down Seventh Avenue, walking toward Times Square. We were amazed how many people were on the street at seven in the evening. While we were enjoying the scenery, suddenly a woman walking behind us started screaming a string of curse words that would make a roughneck blush. When we turned to see who was doing what, it appeared she was looking straight at us or me, and I wondered what I had done wrong. We would soon learn that this was not a rare occurrence. It was enough, however, to turn us in the opposite direction and get us headed back to the hotel.

A couple of blocks later, we stopped at a stoplight before crossing the street. There must have been five hundred people at that intersection, and one of the men was relieving himself in the trash can! We were shocked, first by what he was doing and then by the fact that we were the only ones who were shocked. After we had been there three months, however, I'm afraid almost nothing shocked us! We were glad when that part of our lives was over and we moved into homes with our families.

One of the things that made this move hard on my family was that we had to sell our home in Tulsa. We had moved into this house thinking it would be the largest and most expensive house we would ever own. After all, it cost $25,700! The only way we were able to buy it was that the seller took a second mortgage for $7,000.

What we thought was an enormous price for a house in Tulsa became a pittance compared to what we were seeing in New Jersey. After a month of looking, we had finally bought a house in Morris Plains, New Jersey, for $44,000. We got it for that low price because it was a product of a divorce. It was comical how I eventually got the financing to buy it. None of us who had been transferred had enough money to buy our homes, and the company had made arrangements with Chemical Bank to try their best to provide us with funds. This process was the source of much humor, probably to us more than to them. The guy assigned to listen to our stories could write a book. My conversation went something like this:

CBG (Chemical Bank Guy): I hear you have bought a house?

Me: I will do that as soon as I have the money to close.

CBG: What is the price of the house?

Me: $44,000.

CBG: How much would you like to finance?

Me: All of it.

CBG: We can only do 75 percent on a first mortgage.

Me: I would like a first mortgage for 75 percent of the total amount.

CBG: That's fine. What else can I do for you?

Me: I would like a second for 25 percent.

CBG: I can only do 15 percent on a second.

Me: A 15 percent second sounds good.

CBG: What else can I do for you?

Me: How about a third for 10 percent?

CBG: We are not allowed to do thirds, but nice try!

Me: It has been great doing business with you.

This poor guy had to go through this same experience ten times, almost in the same week. The ten of us compared stories to see if someone had gotten a better deal than the rest of us, but we all had received the same treatment. Because I had very little equity from the sale of our house in Tulsa, I borrowed

$6,000 from Clydella's dad in order to buy the house in Morristown. Our agreement was that I would pay him $34 per month until the debt was satisfied. I had paid him for some twenty years when he said, "Please do not send me any more thirty-four-dollar checks!" So I stopped. I liked doing business with his bank!

I know this may sound like a big promotion, but my salary was only $17,000 per year. I am not sure what the poverty level was at that time, but we were near it. It was not a surprise that our management didn't understand the facts about the cost of living. If you are taking a limo to work every day, you probably don't think about the fact that others are not doing the same. The best buy in that part of the world at the time was a train ticket from Hoboken, New Jersey, to wherever you lived on the Dover branch of the Erie-Lackawanna for $36 per month. If you averaged it, the cost per trip was next to nothing.

Clydella and the boys adapted quickly to their new lives in New Jersey. This was true of every move we made, even the drastic ones like this. However, the first year we were there, Clydella began to have physical symptoms that sent her to the doctor. As you can imagine, this had me quite concerned. In October of that year, 1970, she was diagnosed with type 1 diabetes. What that would involve in her life over the years was not clear to us at the time. Initially, she would go on medication to control the effects of the disease. She was under the care of what we were told was a great doctor, and we had no reason to doubt that, but her condition slowly went downhill over the next three years. She continued to lose weight and did not look healthy.

Despite her health challenges, however, Clydella got involved in many things during our time in New Jersey. One of the most unique was becoming a teacher in the Jewish temple in Morristown. She was only considered because we had become good friends with a dentist and his wife who attended the temple. The wife was almost as powerful as the rabbi, and through her influence, Clydella became one of the kindergarten teachers. She was allowed to do everything but teach about the Jewish holidays. She was even allowed to make an Oklahoma version of chicken soup the day after they had made Jewish chicken soup, which excludes pieces of chicken. They would not allow the class to vote which one was their favorite!

When the First Methodist Church we were attending in Morristown burned to the ground, the temple graciously allowed us to use its facilities since it had little need for them on Sunday. Scott was in the process of going through confirmation class at the time, and at the completion of the course, he was baptized and confirmed in the Methodist church. However, the event took place in the Jewish temple with the rabbi in attendance. Other than the members of his class, I doubt anyone else has had the same experience.

※ ※ ※

It wasn't long after I had committed my business life to the Lord that I realized significant things were happening, not necessarily on the basis of my performance. Early on in 1970, it was evident to me that the purchasing areas I was to combine needed to be some place other than New York City. My choice was Tulsa, and I wrote a report with that conclusion. When I submitted my report to the executive vice president to whom I was reporting, he almost had cardiac arrest.

The management of Cities at that time was headed by two individuals who were sixty-five and sixty-two years old. That seems young to me now, but at the time, they seemed a lot older. These two individuals had no intention of moving the home office anywhere. With that in mind, my boss buried my report very deep in his desk file so that no one could ever know it existed. Two years later, everything changed when both the two older leaders passed away. They were replaced by men who were forty-four and forty-one, and not long after that, I got a call from my boss who asked me to resurrect my study. As a result, we moved the central purchasing department to Tulsa in 1973, which eventually led to the relocation of our entire New York offices to Tulsa in 1974.

It was a blessing when we moved back to Tulsa in 1973 for many reasons, but chief among them was Clydella's health. Under the care of our doctor in New Jersey, she had done nothing but get worse. However, when she first walked into the office of her doctor in Broken Arrow, he took one look at her and immediately put her on insulin. This experience certainly confirmed the importance of second opinions! At 118 pounds and looking very pale, she went into the hospital to transition to using insulin.

While this move saved her life, diabetes is an erratic disease. It is said to be controllable, but the term *control* has a different meaning than what appears in the dictionary. Diabetics have to be the most disciplined people in the world to stay healthy. They have to monitor what they eat along with their physical activities to determine the amount of insulin they need. All of this is very hard to track and nearly impossible to predict. Furthermore, over the years, the disease adversely affects parts of the body, which causes more health problems.

We also discovered that most people did not know what a diabetic goes through. Their response to finding out Clydella was a diabetic was "Funny, you don't look diabetic." I thank God I am married to an exceptional woman! From the beginning, she chose to handle her problem very well. Her faith was the key as it always has been in every situation we have faced together. Although the disease becomes harder to control with age, even today, she is very diligent to stay on top of it as best she can.

By this time, we had decided that Tulsa was our favorite town, and we wanted to retire there when the time came. Unfortunately, we had only been there a year after leaving the New York office, actually 364 days, when I was made general manager of the Onshore Gulf Coast Division, Exploration and Production, in Houston, Texas. So off we went to Houston for about three years, after which we came back to Tulsa in 1977. I was now vice president of the Western Region, US, Exploration and Production, which included the western half of the United States.

In 1979, I was asked to take over the western hemisphere portion of the International Exploration and Production operations. I had the choice to go to Houston, where the offices were, or stay in Tulsa and commute. If I took the former, I would have to come back in about two years. I chose to commute. Less than two years later, I became executive vice president of Planning, Technology, and Services, and the job was in Tulsa. We were grateful that God allowed us to stay where we wanted to be!

* * *

There were a few things I did in every move. First, I always looked around and inevitably discovered some people who were as qualified and/or more deserving of the promotion I had just received. Second, I was never in some of those jobs long enough for anyone, including myself, to know whether or not I had done what I was supposed to do! Third, and most important, I never was impressed with myself when promotions came because I had given my career over to God.

I found that one of the great advantages of placing my professional life in God's hands was that I no longer had to worry about moving up in the corporate system. I simply followed His nudges and worked hard, believing what He said in the Bible: He would not place me in any position I couldn't handle without his assistance, and he always had my (and my family's) best interest in mind. Most of the time, I wondered about my own ability, but that lack of confidence was overshadowed by my faith in Him to provide whatever

I needed. It was a great comfort to know this, and I can look back and see how He came through for me repeatedly with every surprising twist and turn.

One of those surprises came in 1980. Planning, Technology, and Services was new to me. It was a new combination of responsibilities, so it was new to everyone. It was like being responsible for all the things no one else wanted to be responsible for, all rolled into one. One of those tasks was to supervise the group that was responsible for a new fifty-two story building that would house all of Cities's employees in Tulsa. By 1980, we had about 4,400 employees there, occupying space in about ten different buildings. Someone calculated that within a few years we would increase to at least 5,000 employees, which justified the building project. Because my report had been helpful in the relocation of many of these employees from New York City to Tulsa, I had been aware of our growing need for more office space, but I had no desire to get closer to the details. Now, suddenly, the project was mine.

The building was originally estimated to cost $180 million. I found out that this estimate was made before the management team had met with the architect to discuss certain changes. He was in San Francisco, so I immediately flew out to see where we stood. Everything seemed to be in order until I asked what the price of the changes would be. The answer was $100 million. My first thought was that we could not afford that, but I kept it to myself. However, that thought remained after I returned to Tulsa, so I told our CEO what I thought.

Our CEO did not receive my opinion well, and he insisted Cities could afford the building and needed to go forward. Therefore, we proceeded. About three months later, the CEO came into my office and said we could not afford the cost of the building as proposed. I think I said something like, "Is there an echo here? Seems I heard this before." We decided that rather than try to figure out how we could change the design to reduce the cost by $100 million, we would tell the architect what we could spend and see what he could do.

The architect reduced the size of the building from fifty-two to thirty-seven stories. By the time we made this change, the foundation for the taller building was already in the ground. When Occidental bought Cities Service in 1983, which we will talk about later, the building was at sixteen stories. It was quickly sold and is currently the headquarters of ONEOK in Tulsa, and its unusual shape and design stand out among the buildings downtown. At this point, there was never a question in my mind that God was putting me in situations I would only be able to manage with his guidance and wisdom.

Also in 1980, I was asked by the lay leader of our church to give my testimony at our three services on Sunday. While I was always conscious of my relationship with Jesus Christ, I had not been very vocal about it. God impressed on me that if I did give my testimony, then I had better be everything I said I was and believed in. If I wasn't willing to do that, then I should not do it.

I gave my testimony, and as a result, the first thing I did was clean up my language and that only happened with the help of the Holy Spirit! Being raised in the oil field, my language was not complimentary to my testimony. It was really not complimentary to anything. Today, there are people in my life who have known me for many years but have never heard me curse. Giving my testimony inspired me to be even more serious about my commitment to Jesus Christ, and I soon found myself in situations that sorely challenged my new commitment.

When our CEO retired in 1981, Chuck Waidelich became CEO of Cities. Prior to his promotion, I had been asked if I had any desire to become president and COO of the company. At that time, I expressed the desire to head Exploration and Production Operations instead. I knew the person currently in that position wanted to be president, and I knew that was not going to happen. I knew when he wasn't picked for that position, he would leave. As it turned out, I was the only one who thought that. The executive vice president of Refining, Marketing, and Transportation became president instead, and I was asked to fill his position.

All this happened during a very crazy time involving Boone Pickens, Gulf Oil, and Occidental, which I will relate in the next chapter. For right now, just understand that pressure was coming from all sides, and I was in no way happy to be the executive vice president of Refining, Marketing, and Transportation. To make matters worse, during the first quarter of 1982 the head of Exploration and Production Operations left the company. My premonition came true, and I was ready to move into that position and leave a job in which I had no interest. After all, this is what I had requested in the first place.

To my dismay, another person was asked to fill that job, and that person was a good friend. My opposition to his promotion had nothing to do with him personally. I was simply upset that no one had listened to me when I had told them I wanted to lead Exploration and Production.

I proceeded to the new president's office and indicated my surprise and disappointment. He tried to dispel my frustration by saying that I needed to have some experience in Refining, Marketing, and Transportation because I would be president of the company in the not-too-distant future. I reminded him that my desire was to head up oil and gas and not to be president. However, I told him I would not do anything (i.e., quit) without telling them and returned to my office to contemplate my future. On some level, I knew God had to be at work. I just couldn't see it.

As soon as I got to my office, I got a call from Chuck Waidelich. He asked me to meet him for an evening run on the indoor track at Oral Roberts University so we could discuss my reaction to the management change. As I drove out to ORU, the fog was about as bad as I had ever seen it, and it looked like it was going to be there all night. I prayed that God would show me the right decision to make, whatever that might be.

Chuck and I started our run, and immediately, he told me I needed to continue the job at Refining,

Marketing, and Transportation. I needed the experience. I responded that I had no desire to learn more about that business. I found nothing to be gained from trying to run a business while reporting to the guy who had been running it for the last ten years. The results of that kind of relationship are pretty predictable, and it rarely works.

After about a mile of running, Chuck stopped and asked, "Would you do it for me as a favor?"

That was almost not fair. I knew he meant for me to respond yes to his request, and I did. It was hard, but I felt it was the right thing to do. Then, as I walked out of the aerobic center, I saw that the fog had completely lifted and so had all my doubts and anger about remaining at Refining, Marketing, and Transportation. Did God lift the fog to confirm my decision, or was it just a coincidence? It was no coincidence for me!

* * *

Clydella stayed busy primarily with our three boys. All three got involved in soccer while we were in Houston and played until they got out of school. Stuart played soccer in Austin with his older brother until he hurt a knee and had to give it up. Scott, our older son, still plays competitive soccer at the age of fifty-one. I think that is called "for the love of the game!"

When we lived in Houston, Clydella also began a career as a volunteer. She started a kindergarten at our church and volunteered in one of the hospitals there. Her hospital work continued at Saint Francis Hospital in Tulsa when we moved back there. She remains one of the best not-for-profit board members in the city. Currently, she is still on the board of about five not-for-profits and one foundation. In most respects, her career is more successful than my own.

With all this moving around, I know that after the boys were grown, they were glad they could live where they wanted. With each move, I tried to explain that they were being put in a position of greater advantage in their lives, that their experiences would be more diverse than many kids, and I think they understood that and valued it somewhat. I also presume that the moves had no long-lasting, negative effect on them. Two of them never wanted to be a part of a large corporation, which may have been a result of their upbringing, but overall, especially with Clydella's great attitude, our family took the moves in stride.

2
BOONE PICKENS A-01

Some people get their MBA in school, but some of us achieve the same thing in the business world. I would suspect that the former is easier than the latter, but it certainly isn't as much fun. My first course toward a master's in business administration began near the end of my 1980 job with Planning, Technology, and Services and extended into the latter part of 1982. During this time, I became executive vice president of Refining, Marketing, and Transportation, the job I didn't want. The course was taught by none other than Boone Pickens, who at that time had built up an oil and gas company, Mesa Petroleum. While he was known in the industry at the time, his actions over the next few years would make him famous in some eyes, infamous in others.

LESSON 1:
HELLO, CORPORATE RAIDERS

Early in 1981, Boone bought about five percent of the stock of Cities Service Company. At the same time, a Canadian company also bought the same amount of stock. When ten percent of our stock was suddenly bought by two entities, who had no perceived interest in the company long-term, it created a large problem. Shareholders of Cities were lead to believe that the price of the stock was undervalued and something needed to be done to correct the situation. Their intention, at least Boone's, was to put the company on the auction block and see where that would go. The Canadian company did not stay long as a shareholder because it became apparent to them that they were out of their league.

Boone bought our stock at about $30 per share, which attracted other buyers and enticed Cities's stockholders to become interested in increasing the value of their stock through any action including the sale of the company. Subsequently, the combination of the perceived undervalued stock, and the stockholders' openness to see that change, put Cities in play. That made Boone happy, of course. When someone was successful in seeing this approach work to put a company in play to be sold in an open auction, the profits made, as a result of the transaction, were called "green mail" and the people involved were called "corporate raiders."

All of this is perfectly legal when you are dealing with a publicly owned company. Anyone who has the money can buy stock and put this process in motion when the perceived value of the stock is much higher than the market. In our industry, this was happening because of the cycle of oil prices that has existed over the years. When the cycle is high in price, everything is fine. When they are low, the company is undervalued, at least perceived to be. So enter the raiders!

However, this was a new experience to me and to Cities Service. It was upsetting because corporate raiders were not long-term owners. What happened in the long run to our company was not important to them. If they bought low and sold high, they would walk away with a nice profit. In the meantime, our company would either have been sold to the highest bidder, which would involve being absorbed into another company (with a large loss of jobs) or broken into asset groups and sold to interested parties.

Since the issues raised by this series of events were new to the management of Cities, and even to the oil industry in the early 1980s, we immediately sought counsel on how to respond. We were not totally in the dark as to the process that would be pursued, mainly because we had on our board two members from large New York banks and one member from a large investment banking firm. They advised us to acquire the services of corporate takeover lawyers and investment bankers. We had almost no experience in dealing with these groups either.

Working with these firms was an eye-opener. Your initial assumption is that the people you become involved with are on your side, especially if you are paying them to look out for your interests. The more experience you have in the process, however, the more you begin to question that assumption! Nevertheless, we moved forward to try to determine what action was appropriate under the circumstances.

Because the Canadian company sold their shares very quickly after they bought them, they didn't make a big profit. Boone held on to his and Cities Service remained intact, but our equilibrium had been challenged. We determined to keep our eyes open, and as it turned out, there was a lot to see. We didn't have to wait long before the next development.

※ ※ ※

LESSON 2: EXPECT THE UNEXPECTED

Lesson two began with an action taken by another company, which had no direct effect on us yet. Early in the year, Dome Petroleum, a Canadian company, approached Conoco with an offer to buy Hudson Bay, Conoco's Canadian operation. The CEO of Dome was a man named Jack Gallagher, and he was the reason Dome made such a brazen proposition to a company much larger in size and history. US companies did not know Gallagher very well. That would change very quickly, and it certainly did for Conoco. I do not know what the *tone* of Conoco's response to Dome was, but they told Gallagher they had no desire to sell Hudson Bay to Dome or anyone else.

At the time of Gallagher's proposition, Ralph Bailey was the CEO of Conoco, a long-standing company that was well thought of by everyone in the industry. Cities had been partners with Conoco for many years in a variety of projects, especially in the Gulf of Mexico, and we liked doing business with them. That being said, Ralph Bailey and Conoco were not ready for what happened next.

Led by Gallagher, after the turndown, Dome tendered in the open market for twenty five percent of Conoco's stock. Their intention was to acquire the twenty five percent and then trade the shares back to Conoco in exchange for Hudson Bay. This was a legal but hostile way to take the issue out of management's hands and let the stockholders decide. It would be interesting to know whether Dome was prepared from the beginning to carry out this alternate approach to acquire Hudson Bay. The speed by which the tender offer was made after Conoco turned them down led us to believe they were.

It was certainly not apparent that the contest between Conoco and Dome would have any impact on Cities. How could Conoco's problems create any problems for us? We seemed to have enough on our plate dealing with Boone Pickens. However, what happened next was very disconcerting to us. Dome's tender was so successful that not only did the shareholders tender 25 percent of the stock, but in the end, a total of 53 percent was tendered altogether. The Conoco shareholders had wanted to enhance the value of their stock so much, they were willing to sell a controlling interest in the company. Dome then traded their 25 percent for Hudson Bay. I never understood why Dome did not increase their tender and buy the controlling interest in the company. This transaction frightened Conoco, and their stock was truly undervalued.

Back at Cities, we were concerned by the Dome-Conoco bout, but we were more consumed with keeping track of what Boone, our largest individual shareholder, was doing. At this point, we knew we had to be alert. Things were changing, and we had to be ready to respond to these changes. Even so, we had no thought that the results of the Dome-Conoco transaction would have an impact on us. Then the phone rang. It was Ralph Bailey, and the question he put to us was "Would you have any interest in merging with Conoco?"

The executive management of Cities pondered the question. If we pursued discussions with Conoco and the sale did not go through, would we put ourselves in play for an eventual sale? As we evaluated this, the answer to that question became apparent. Who were we kidding? The recent large purchases of stock had already put us in play! We were reluctant players, but nonetheless players. At least, we knew Conoco. Or we thought we did The merger could work out well for both parties. We decided to go for it and answered yes. Thus began three months of working toward an acceptable deal for both parties.

Our work progressively defined the equitable conditions we were both seeking. There appeared to be an agreement as to the value of assets, so members of the management of the two companies headed to New York City. Over the next twenty-four hours, we worked almost full time, with the help of attorneys and investment bankers from both sides. Finally, we reached an agreement on the details of the merger, so a press release could be prepared. The CEOs, Ralph Bailey of Conoco and Chuck Waidelich of Cities, were near the end of that task when something would take place that was a total surprise to Cities, less of a surprise to Conoco.

AN MBA THE HARD WAY

In the early 1980s when this took place, there were no laptops, cell phones, Internet, or e-mail. Back then, there were no car wrecks due to texting or talking on cell phones. We found other reasons to have wrecks. To find out what was going on in the stock market, you had to watch the ticker tape from Dow Jones. It was the Twitter of that age.

As we reached an agreement about the final wording of the press release to the public, the ticker tape interrupted our discussions. Seagram, the Canadian company that produced alcoholic beverages, was making a hostile tender for all the stock of Conoco at $75 per share. I do not remember whether Seagram had any interest in oil and gas at that time, which made their tender even less understandable, at least to us.

With little discussion, we deemed it reasonable for Cities to get out of the fight and quietly go home, which we did. We appreciated the opportunity we had been offered but saw no benefit to going on with the deal. After we returned home, we discussed whether or not that had been a wise decision, but we never came to a solid conclusion.

From afar, we watched additional players enter the contest to acquire Conoco, and our eyes were opened. Seagram was required by law to issue a proxy statement as to the particulars in their offer for Conoco. The details of their proxy statement shocked the management of Cities to our core. At the same time Conoco had opened discussions with us to merge, they had also entered into parallel discussions with Seagram to buy Conoco. Neither Seagram nor Cities knew that the other party was involved.

The rules of the game we thought we knew had changed. We could no longer count on full disclosure during business dealings such as these. I tend to believe the idea for Conoco to run parallel discussions with both Cities and Seagram originated with their investment bankers. They needed to complete a deal, and the money associated with the deal overwhelmed the rules of the game formerly considered sacred.

I will take this opportunity, appropriately under the subhead of "Expect the Unexpected", to comment on the rules of the game in the business world. Hopefully, integrity and ethical values are still known and followed by most of those running our businesses and corporations today. The first rule has always been that the management of a company will set and enforce those rules binding all involved to honesty and legal conduct. Unfortunately, some conveniently forget their ethical responsibilities and become more concerned with personal gain.

All that said, I have observed through the years that in the long run, it pays to play by the rules because what goes around comes around. For me, that meant doing things by the book, which allowed me to maintain a clear conscience. Others did not fare so well in this area. The experience of Enron, WorldCom, and other major corporations illustrated to the world the Bible verse, "Be sure your sin will find you out."

What happened to us at Cities during the final stages of discussing the merger with Conoco took us aback, to say the least. How could people we had been so close to for years deceive us in such a manner? I guess they considered corporate survival more important than good relationships. At that time, I could not conceive that Cities would do the same thing in similar circumstances.

In the end, Dupont purchased Conoco for $120 per share in a full-scale market auction, which made their management and shareholders extremely happy. It pleased the employees of Conoco because the Conoco organization would remain intact as a separate division of Dupont, and it also confirmed that the market thought that all oil stocks were undervalued.

LESSON 3:
RELATIONSHIPS MATTER

Relationships can mean the difference between success and failure. Sometimes, the friends you make over the years pop up at the most fortuitous times. For example, in the mid-seventies, I had been general manager for the onshore Gulf of Mexico region of Cities and had met a guy named Jim Beavers from Hunt Oil Company in Fort Worth. Jim Beavers had been a land man and close associate of H. L. Hunt and, at the time, was working for Ray Hunt. We became friends as well as business associates, and as a result, Hunt funded many of the wells in our program for the year 1975 when we were strapped for funds as a result of overspending the budget for lease sales in the Gulf of Mexico. I am not sure that the success of the wells to Hunt was enough to justify his friendship to me, but I always enjoyed doing business with him.

Fast-forward six years to 1981, just after our adventures with Conoco. I was head-over-heels–overwhelmed by all of the things going on around us when I got a call from Jim, whom I had not seen or heard from in about three years. He said he was in Tulsa and wanted to see how I was doing. After we exchanged pleasantries, I said, "Jim, I know you've been in Tulsa many times over the last couple of years and didn't call, so what's up? Why now?"

I sensed his hesitation, and then he said he had heard via the grapevine that the following Monday, Boone Pickens was going to make a hostile tender for 100 percent of Cities's stock. I was not that surprised because we knew this was his ultimate goal, but I felt I should ask, "Who's involved?"

Jim replied that rumor had it that Mesa, Boone's company, Freeport McMoran, Louisiana Land and Exploration, and Mark Production, a German company, were each participating for 25 percent. By way of our friendship and Jim's history with some of those players, I knew without asking that his sources were reliable. I also knew that if I hadn't asked the right questions, he would not have said a thing. I thanked him for his information.

It was Thursday, and Jim had said Boone and his partners were going to act on Monday, so I immediately went to see Chuck Waidelich. I related what I knew and stressed the need for action. He questioned the validity of the information and rightly so. I answered that it was my opinion that the information was exactly what was going down. He immediately picked up the phone and called the CEO of Louisiana Land and Exploration and indicated to him that we were aware of the deal he had made. He also said that if they were part of the Monday tender for Cities, we would tender for 100 percent of Louisiana Land and Exploration before the day was out. Their CEO disclaimed any knowledge of any such thing.

Chuck had the same conversation with the CEO of Freeport McMoran, and both companies decided to drop their participation in the upcoming tender. Boone's deal fell through. Three years later, a deposition involving Pickens confirmed that the deal we were able to squelch was real and would have taken place had we not acted preemptively. Because of my friendship with Jim Beavers, Cities dodged a Boone Pickens bullet and I learned how valuable good relationships could be.

LESSON 4: DON'T BE NAÏVE

The year 1981 ended and we were glad to see it go. We thought things could not get any worse. The following year would prove our naiveté. I can honestly say that if we had taken a management survey about what we thought could happen during 1982, no one would have been close. To begin with, Boone tried another tactic. Mesa Petroleum tendered for 25 percent of Cities Service stock. Boone had given up bringing other partners into the play. I also believe the only reason he did this was to become enough of a nuisance that we would buy back his stock for a higher price.

Our response was different than what Boone expected, however. Shortly after he tendered for 25 percent of Cities's stock, we tendered for 100 percent of Mesa Petroleum. Boone later explained what went on in an article in *Texas Monthly* in 1982. While we proceeded to move in that direction and he searched for an answer to our actions, something else occurred that expanded the game for both of us.

After the Conoco-Seagram episode and the benefit to its shareholders, other companies decided they needed to take action in order to become bigger and more attractive, in some cases bigger and uglier. During this time, the management of Gulf Oil Company felt pressure from its shareholders. In June 1982, they approached us with a deal to acquire Cities for $63 per share. Since they were not looking for a hostile takeover, they approached Chuck Waidelich to see if we would be open to such a deal. Because of all the other things that were up in the air, most of which were beyond our control, we decided to accept the offer.

Immediately, we began the process of discussing with Gulf's team how the merger would take place. This had the added advantage of letting Boone know he was getting further and further from controlling what was going on at Cities. He soon realized that with Gulf in the picture, he could not mount a serious offer or find anyone to partner with him. He probably also wondered about our tender offer for Mesa. Personally, I had no sympathy for Boone; at the price Gulf offered, he still would make a lot of money off the deal.

I led the Cities's transition team that would orchestrate what was necessary to complete the Gulf deal and achieve the reorganization. At the outset, the tenor of the meetings was very cordial. It seemed that Cities would have some say as to our part in the new organization. Another very naïve thought. As we progressed ever so slowly, things happened and information was uncovered that changed the picture almost daily. I was continually reminded that this was not a done deal!

Then Boone Pickens's stock position in Cities became a matter of discussion between the CEOs. Gulf did not like the thought that if their deal with us was completed, Pickens would own a position in Gulf. Their first requirement for Cities was that we purchase Pickens's stock, which we agreed to do. This decision would create legal problems that were not finalized for years to come. It would also come back to haunt Gulf. Eventually, Boone would make a run for Gulf that would result in there being no Gulf Oil Company today.

In response to their request, we repurchased Boone's stock at about fifty-five dollars per share. He made millions of dollars over and above his cost. Not a bad deal for a fifteen-month investment! It would be the catalyst for many similar moves on his part in the future. In retrospect, if the Gulf deal had gone through and had included Boone's position, the subsequent actions by him against Gulf, Philips, and UNOCAL might never have taken place. Just a thought! But at least he was out of our hair, and we were out of his.

In the end, our deal with Gulf did not go through. What surfaced very quickly was that Gulf's board members were not unanimously agreed on the purchase of Cities Service. There was a distinct and powerful minority that was becoming very public in their opposition. Some of them represented the founding family of Gulf Oil, so their opposition was formidable, and yet we were only indirectly aware of it. We continued negotiations as if nothing was happening.

The first time we clearly saw the opposition was during discussions between the transition teams. About three weeks in, the tone of the meetings took a nosedive when a new player entered the scene. It would be my first encounter with a person named Hammer. Harold Hammer was the leader of the opposition contingent on Gulf's board. He joined the meeting, and all the rules changed. Gulf was no longer negotiating; they were calling the shots. Furthermore, according to Mr. Hammer, Cities's personnel would have no part in the new corporation. We soon realized Hammer was against the deal and would do everything in his power to cause it to evaporate. He was not a reasonable man, and it became apparent he was also the main fly in the ointment of the CEO of Gulf.

The next revelation came when Gulf engaged a legal firm from Chicago that was "expert" in dealing with agencies in Washington, DC. These agencies needed to approve our acquisition. The law firm's strategy was to take positions for their client that were opposite to the requests coming out of Washington. Moreover, they would agree to no concessions and were rigidly uncompromising. Hiring this firm was another indication that the deal was not going to be done.

Unfortunately, at this point, there was little we could do. Since Gulf's tender, Cities's stock had gone from roughly $30 per share to about $60 per share, and a good portion of the stock was in the hands of arbitragers, or traders, which was normal. We had to proceed as if we didn't understand the implications of Gulf's opposition strategy. Finally, in July of 1982, Gulf reneged on their offer.

The market response to Gulf's withdrawal and the collapse of our merger sent Cities's stock back to $30 per share, which put the traders in trouble. They were now in the red on a deal they thought was done. As for our board, we soon discovered the full meaning of the term *conflict of interest*. They were a very talented group, made up of CEOs and leaders of major corporations and banks as well as other gifted and capable people. They would stand up under the scrutiny of anyone, but we never could have anticipated the pressure the withdrawal of Gulf would put them under.

Among our board members were a CEO of a major international bank, a vice chairman of a similar bank, and a CEO and founder of one of the largest investment banks, each a source of funding to the traders who held our stock! As a result of Gulf's departure, their businesses became troubled, and of course, their first allegiance was to their companies, not Cities. This situation was so grave that the board decided to put all Cities's assets collectively or separately on the market. They did this to prop up the value of the stock as much as possible. The turmoil this action caused our company still remains a source of discomfort for me, even after all these years.

By far, the most difficult challenge during this time was our inability to properly communicate to employees what was going on and what the outcome would be. During our negotiations with Gulf, we could not, in good conscience, guarantee that our employees would retain their jobs after the deal was done, and after the deal collapsed, their job security was even less predictable. We did not know which assets would be sold and to whom. I tried to get to work earlier than anyone and go home later. That way I would avoid seeing people in the elevator! I had no encouraging words nor could I explain what was happening. I couldn't explain it because I wasn't sure myself.

For several weeks, we entertained, using the word loosely, any and all individuals or companies that wanted to cherry-pick the best assets of the company. There were a few discussions that were legitimate, but most were not worth the time we spent making presentations. However, it seemed to be necessary to treat them all the same. In the end, the only discussion that was at all serious was with Southland Corporation of Dallas. The time spent with them would prove to be time well spent for both parties later.

In the end, it was another Hammer that managed to save Cities. While my memories of Harold Hammer of Gulf's board were not pleasant, Occidental Petroleum, whose CEO was Dr. Armand Hammer, approached us with an offer. It was not as high as the Gulf offer, but it beat all of the goofy things we were hearing in our asset sale discussions. Fortunately, none of those sales had been consummated, and on August 2, 1982, Occidental tendered for 100 percent of Cities's stock at $52 per share, with full cooperation from the management team at Cities.

LESSON 5: GOD IS JUST

Although Gulf's withdrawal came as no surprise to us, we had one big bone to pick with them. We had lost about $250 million in assets because they had required us to buy back Boone Pickens's stock at the higher price. Therefore, on August 6, 1982, we filed a lawsuit against Gulf in Tulsa, suing them for damages.

In the meantime, Pickens made a run for Gulf Oil, which resulted in the purchase of Gulf by Chevron in a market auction. Thus, Chevron inherited our lawsuit against Gulf. I will spare you the details of how that suit progressed; suffice it to say that some fourteen years later, and after some brilliant legal expertise led by DeVier Pierson and supported by a bevy of other lawyers, especially our Tulsa outside attorney Oliver Howard, a settlement of this issue was reached. My definition of *great legal counsel* involves much of what I learned from DeVier and Oliver. The details of this legal battle between Occidental-Cities and Chevron-Gulf are a part of DeVier's book, *Special Counsel*, which came out in 2009. In the end, we received a settlement payment of $742 million.

The interesting thing that is not known by many is that the lawsuit could have been settled within two years, in 1984. Bob Abboud, president of Occidental and my new boss, asked me to negotiate a quick settlement. We needed the cash, and Abboud did not put much faith in a suit that would not be decided for years. As an executive of Occidental, he had not had the privilege of going through the debacle with Gulf.

A couple weeks later, I had the opportunity to spend a weekend with Ken Derr, who at the time was in charge of the integration of Gulf's assets into Chevron. Shortly after that, he became Chevron's CEO and served for some years. During our weekend of golf and fellowship, I broached the subject of settling the existing lawsuit. For reasons unknown to us, Ken indicated that he was not aware of the suit or the issues involved.

In the end, Gulf ceased to exist, and we were reimbursed by Chevron for our capital loss during our negotiations with Gulf. After it was all over, I looked back and remembered that God is not only merciful, but just.

There were so many things I learned from these first experiences that began and ended with Boone Pickens in the mix. I would like to say that in all cases, I adhered to this wisdom, but I would be lying!

Here are the most important:

- Keep your eyes open. Pay attention to what's going on. Consider carefully every conversation, as there may be more behind what is being said than meets the eye. (The Bible calls that discernment.)
- Expect the unexpected.

- Ask the right questions.
- Don't be naïve. Remember that some people and companies are out for themselves and don't care what happens to you or your company.
- One of the best defense mechanisms you have is a loyal friend, a wonderful gift.

GOING UPSTREAM

The Occidental Petroleum (Oxy) phase of my life is still prevalent in my thoughts today. After the Gulf deal failed, we needed a white knight to save us from the terrible fate of being cut into pieces and sold off. Oxy showed up and tendered their offer to buy us, and we were especially glad to see them! However, I knew very few people in their organization and nothing about Armand Hammer, the CEO.

One of the first things I learned was that our new CEO liked to be called "Doctor." As a young man, he had graduated from Columbia Physicians and Surgical School and was selected for an internship at Bellevue Hospital in New York City, but he had to wait six months to begin the program. During that delay, he went to Russia to help with the disease and famine that had occurred after the revolution. As a result, his career went an entirely different direction.

By the time I met Dr. Hammer, he was a very successful businessman who was known throughout the world. I was immediately thrown together with him, and for the next eight years, I was to discover a lot more about him.

When Oxy came on the scene, I was executive vice president of Refining, Marketing, and Transportation, which meant I was responsible for the downstream business. *Downstream* involves everything that gets the product from the production location to the refinery and then gasoline and other products to the market. Occidental was an upstream company, and *upstream* involves finding the oil or gas, producing it, and getting it to a sales point. Occidental had been successful in Libya and was known to be an international company.

Occidental had no downstream activities and also no desire to enter that side of the business. That was agreeable to me because, although I had been running Cities's downstream business for about seven months, I wanted to get back into the upstream side of things. As you may recall, I had told the management of Cities Service that I wanted to be president of Exploration and Production. You could say I wanted to go upstream, and the first thing Oxy did about that was to sell the part of the company I led: Refining, Marketing, and Transportation. That business is what you may currently know as CITGO.

* * *

Although they paid about $10 per share lower than the Gulf offer, the price Oxy paid for Cities was a substantial premium over market price. Interestingly, Oxy was a smaller company than Cities in market capitalization, production, and reserves. Therefore, they needed to sell some assets to cover their costs in purchasing us, and it was obvious that the business I was running would be the first to go. My job security, however, was not in question.

During the last couple of months of our negotiations with Gulf, Cities offered six of us the opportunity to sign five-year contracts in case there were changes in ownership. These contracts would soon be known as "golden parachutes," and I do not think they existed in the industry prior to this time. We did not sign the documents during the Gulf fiasco. In fact, we thought we would never sign them until Oxy tendered to buy us and we knew this deal would go through. Management of Oxy encouraged us to sign, so our contracts would be part of the deal with them. Sign we did.

Our contracts required that we stay for the first year, and then, at our discretion, we could leave and be paid for the next four years. With that fallback position and knowing I was not in charge of the process, because God was, I continued to do my job at Refining, Marketing, and Transportation. I didn't have to wait long for my first orders from Oxy: "We don't want the downstream business. Find someone to buy CITGO."

One of the six of us who had contracts, the president of Cities, did not like those orders or the way Oxy conducted business in general. His attitude soon brought him into conflict with Dr. Hammer, and then he made some disparaging remarks about Oxy in a meeting. After that, he was no longer part of the long-term plans of the combined companies. What this meant for the rest of us was still not clear.

The search for a buyer for the downstream business began, and as head of that business, I was part of that search. I traveled with Dr. Hammer to Abu Dhabi, Qatar, Bahrain, Kuwait, and Mexico, where we talked with the leaders of those countries to see if they had any interest. This was the first time I was in a position to see the doctor operate. His access to people was unequaled.

I also attempted discussions with a lot of people, including Marc Rich. I had met Marc about three years before, during a gala to raise money for diabetes research. Marvin and Barbara Davis, whose daughter was diabetic, held the gala every year. Marvin was the founder and owner of Davis Oil Company, who partnered with Cities Service in many of the wells we drilled in the Rocky Mountains. Since we shared this terrible disease with the Davises and many others, Clydella and I began attending the gala. We were always overwhelmed by who was in attendance. This was especially true after Marvin bought Twentieth Century Fox with Marc Rich.

One year Clydella and I found ourselves at a table with Marc Rich and his wife. We had no idea who they were and vice versa, but we had a very pleasant conversation that happened to avoid discussing what we did to earn a living. Later, when Dr. Hammer and I were trying to find a buyer for the downstream business, I was unaware that Marc Rich was under investigation by the US government for certain irregularities.

Entering the Helmsley Palace Hotel in New York one day, I ran into Marc. I had not seen him since the gala and was so consumed with my own problem that I asked him if he had any interest in discussing the possibility of buying our downstream business. He tactfully indicated that he would have no time to do that. Shortly thereafter, he left the country and, as far as I know, has never been back, even though he was pardoned by President Clinton.

There were other more comical times during my search for buyers. One day, I received a registered letter from a foreign company. The letter read, "This is an unconditional letter of intent to purchase your downstream business for $1 billion." I asked our general counsel about the validity of it, and he made some reference to what is commonly used in every bathroom. I felt obliged to follow up just in case there might be some opportunity there, but in the end the meeting was a waste of time.

That brings us to Southland Corporation, who had looked at our assets before Oxy had shown up. They owned many businesses, including the 7-Eleven convenience store operation, which included over 11,000 convenience stores. Southland had been one of our more serious possibilities during the asset sale fiasco, when I had met with their representative, Sam Susser. Later, when it looked like Oxy would acquire Cities, I called Sam and said, "Oxy will not want this downstream business. Hang tight, and we will be in discussions before you know it. If you are looking to get into this business, this is by far the best opportunity available." I am not a prophet, but I could recognize a mutually beneficial opportunity.

Southland was run by two brothers, John and Jerry Thompson. A third brother, Jody, was not a part of the management team but was a part owner. Their father, Joe, had founded the company, which had expanded from an ice company to a very large purchaser and retailer of gasoline through the 7-Eleven outlets. My recollection is that during our first talks with them, they were purchasing about 125,000 barrels of gasoline per day. They were nice guys and ran a very successful business. They would also prove to be very tough negotiators.

The first phase was a meeting early in February 1983 in Dallas at the Southland offices. There were about twelve of us present, including John, Jerry, Jody, Dr. Hammer, and Bob Abboud. The meeting began with a dinner and general talk about our businesses and the assets in question. Eventually, John, Jerry, Dr. Hammer, Abboud, and Southland's general counsel and investment banker went into a private session. When they came out a couple of hours later, they had agreed to the basic elements of a letter of intent for Southland to purchase CITGO.

Jerry Stern, the general counsel of Oxy, and I were told we would be meeting the following day with some of the Southland people to finalize a formal LOI and then proceed to the details of a stock purchase agreement. With that general instruction, the big players left. Dr. Hammer and Bob Abboud returned to Los Angeles without any comment to Jerry or me regarding what had gone on in the meeting or a plan we were to pursue. Thus, Stern and I had no idea what to expect.

The next day at our first meeting, Oxy was represented by Stern, another lawyer, and myself. Southland was represented by Sam Susser, their general counsel, their investment banker, and one other person.

At least two of Southland's people had been present at the private meeting the night before. No one on our team had that advantage, which made for a very interesting discussion. They proceeded to tell us what everyone had agreed to, the deal being built around a purchase price of about $1 billion. This amount could be increased or decreased through due diligence and a very specific inventory of oil and gas products in the system.

The next item was a bombshell. Since much of Cities's oil and gas upstream production was easily accessible to the pipelines of the downstream business, Southland wanted the right to purchase up to 80,000 barrels of oil per day of crude for fifteen years, the pricing system to be agreed on by both parties to ensure that it represented market price. I almost fell out of my chair. In the days to come, much was said about this issue, and I conferred with Dr. Hammer to try and understand how firm this commitment was. It was soon apparent to me that as far as Dr. Hammer was concerned, the deal was done the night he left the meeting in Dallas. I was to fill in the details, and if I needed help, find it.

As long as the pricing basis ensured we would get a market price for the oil being sold, this deal was acceptable; nevertheless, to do such a thing was like joining us at the hip with someone who was not our brother, and we were asking for legal problems for some time to come. The years proved that this was to be very true.

It was then that the investment banker for Southland dropped the real bombshell. He claimed that Dr. Hammer had promised them a discount on the oil that would be purchased over the next fifteen years. He hinted that the discount from market price was fifty cents per barrel. My calculator told me quickly that this amounted to $219 million. My position from that point until the issue was decided was, "Maybe that's what you heard him say, but that is not what he meant."

This was by far the biggest sale I had been responsible for, and sometimes, the enormity of it bothered me. To compound the situation, I was new to the Oxy organization and did not know how things worked there. Knowing how management thinks and what their primary concerns are is vital when you are negotiating a transaction for them. It was more than a year later before I began to understand what was going on at Oxy and why things happened the way they did. The revelation was somewhere between comical and instructional.

We completed the letter of intent, and Stern and I continued toward the stock purchase agreement, at times feeling as though our eyes were blindfolded and our hands were tied behind our backs by not knowing what happened in the meeting. We had to formulate and complete the documents necessary to close a billion-dollar-plus deal, which in 1983 was enormous. Then Southland brought in a young lawyer from New York to lead their discussions. Immediately, he and I were at odds over almost everything. For every step we would take forward, we took two backward.

Jerry Stern and I could not understand the sudden disconnect, and every time I would bring up the subject to Susser, his eyes would glaze over and no explanation was given. It was almost two months into this process, and after losing a lot of sleep, that it finally hit me what was going on. I was irritated that Southland hadn't just told us what their problem was because it was very easy to resolve.

At our refinery in Lake Charles, Louisiana, which was a key asset in their purchase of CITGO, we had a major construction project underway to build another large coker, a major piece of refining equipment that would allow the refinery to take larger volumes of lower gravity crude oil. It was cheaper to purchase but more difficult to refine, and process the oil to a maximum amount of gasoline. The installation's financial performance was enhanced by the much lower price of the lower gravity crude it processed, and it was a very important part of Southland's purchase.

This project was scheduled to be completed some time in July of 1983. At the normal pace of our negotiations, we would complete the stock purchase agreement and close the deal before the coker was completed and tested. Of course, Southland did not want to sign the agreement until the coker was ready for business. Thus, they brought in a lawyer to delay our progress. He was a lot of things, but mainly obnoxious. When I realized what he was trying to accomplish by all this, however, we simply put the closing of the deal and the completion of the coker on the same schedule.

The stonewalling stopped, and the deal began to move forward again.

* * *

Sam Susser and I became good friends during the negotiations, even as we tried to get the best of each other. We would meet frequently during each week as we progressed to what we hoped would be a final closing, each fighting fiercely for the deal he thought was right. We would yell at each other in a room full of silent lawyers. On occasion, we would meet in private at the end of the week and pick out which one of us deserved the Oscar for that week.

The Southland office was like a campus with an atrium in the middle, and there was a fountain in the center of the courtyard. When Sam and I would tire listening to our lawyers carry on about an issue that needed to be decided, we would go out in the courtyard in full view of our groups and pitch quarters. When we came back in, we had decided the issue. No one knew whether our decision was based on merit or on who won the coin-pitching contest.

* * *

The following story will give you some idea as to the negotiating capabilities of Mr. Susser. He and I scheduled a business trip to New York City to meet with the oil minister of Mexico and to look at a couple of terminals in New Jersey. The trip happened to include the day of his wife's birthday, so Pat went with us. While we were checking in to the Helmsley Palace

Hotel, now called the New York Palace Hotel, Pat was window-shopping in a very exclusive jewelry store, which used to be in the lobby. She called Sam over to show him a cabochon amethyst ring surrounded by diamonds, and conveyed to him that it would make a great birthday present. He was not all that excited about her "suggestion."

After we finished our meeting the following day, Sam said, "Why don't we go look in the jewelry store at the hotel?" As we walked into the store, it did not take much discernment to know that Sam and the lady running the store had done battle before.

She (stone-faced): "Hello, Mr. Susser."

Sam: "There is this costume jewelry ring in the window I would like to see, the one with the purple stone with the rhinestones around it."

She: "That ring is not the most expensive ring we have in the store, but it is by the finest designer in the country."

Sam: "I don't want to know its history. Just what is the price?"

She retrieved the ring and said, "The price is $7,200."

Sam: "You must be out of your mind. I will give you $2500 for it."

She: "I could not possibly do that."

This battle continued for a few minutes more before Sam shrugged his shoulders and we walked outside to the car. By that time, she was down to $3,200 and he was up to $2,600.

As we approached the car, he asked me, "Do you think she would take $2,700?"

I answered, "This negotiation is way beyond my level of expertise, and now I want to go back and renegotiate everything we agreed to so far on the purchase of CITGO!"

Sam proceeded to write out a check for $2,700, and we went back into the store.

She: "I cannot take less than $2,950. Please write me another check."

Sam: "I have no other check," and he showed her his checkbook, no checks remaining, which I thought was a plant he carried for times like these.

She: "Then use your credit card to pay the difference."

Sam: "I don't carry plastic." I didn't believe this at all.

She: "I will take cash."

Sam opened his wallet and showed her one $5 bill, one $10 bill, and one $20 bill.

She reached into his wallet, snatched the $20 bill, and said, "Sold."

Sam bought a $7,200 ring for $2,720. I was astounded. I also could not wait for my next jewelry purchase! When I was able to take advantage of this lesson, it worked to perfection. You now understand the kind of atmosphere surrounding my negotiations with Sam Susser and Southland as we worked on the sale of CITGO to them.

The end to our labors was in sight in July 1983. We set July 30 for the signing of the stock purchase agreement. Two weeks before that date, I took a team of about fifty people to Houston, and Southland did the same. Each of us employed outside law firms that were based there, so this took us to neutral ground for our final push. The main task was that all of the exhibits and contracts to be included in the stock purchase agreement had to be finished before the signing. Sam and I also had almost fifty items we had to agree to before we showed up in Dallas for the signing. We met most of each day during the two weeks to decrease the number of items.

Along with our punch list, we were constantly mediating arguments between our attorneys. I forget how many lawyers we had in place, but it was apparent we had too many. One time, Sam and I walked into the middle of a loud argument when both of us were severely sleep-deprived. We discovered the issue being discussed was valued at only $250,000. I took out a quarter and said, "Sam, you call it."

One of the Oxy lawyers said, "You can't do that."

With the looks Sam and I gave him, he decided we could. I forgot what the outcome was, but that was how we made that decision.

There was only one item that loomed foremost in our minds because neither of us was giving an inch. That was the supposed discount Dr. Hammer had allegedly promised Southland. We seemed to purposely delay that issue as long as we could. As we got into the final stretch, the issue of the discount had to be settled. I was constantly reminded, "That is what the doctor said," to which I consistently responded, "That is not what he meant." Never during the six months of negotiations did I ask Dr. Hammer what he said because I was pretty sure what the answer would be. I knew that a discount was not in order, and I was positive he never meant that.

On Monday, before the stock purchase agreement was to be signed on Thursday, I told Southland that we could not grant any discount on the sale of crude oil. We must have market price or there was no deal, and I walked out of the room. Only then, with the threat of calling off the whole deal, did Sam accept the fact that there would be no discount. That appeared to be the last big issue in the discussions. It wasn't.

I got a call from Bob Abboud, who said Dr. Hammer had just hired a new man to run Oxy's chemical business, and I needed to talk to him. I told Bob I had just cleared the last hurdle in the sale, and I did not need anything to cause a problem. He repeated that I should call the new man, Ray Irani, and listen to his request. I was not looking forward to this phone conversation for the following reason: on the refinery site were a number of chemical plants that had been operated by Cities for some years. They were so unsuccessful that we were making them part of the Southland deal, even though Southland had no use for them. The only way I got Sam to take them was by showing him there might be some salvage value over and above the cost to dismantle them. With this in mind and with great reluctance, I called Ray Irani.

Ray's request was simple: don't make those plants a part of the deal. He wanted to look at them and see if we could use them in the chemical business. I explained the unsuccessful financial history of the plants and that they were already in the deal that was targeted to be closed on Thursday, three days away. In that first conversation, I received tremendous insight into the personality of Ray Irani. He simply demanded, if not yelled, "Do not sell those plants!"

As I went back into the room with Sam and indicated that I want to take the chemical plant assets out of the deal, I would see his ears go to point. I had to be ready. The value of those assets would not have gone up to Southland, but I knew there would be a price.

Everything happened as I thought. I walked in and said, "I want to pull the chemical plants out of the deal." Immediately, I could see Sam's mind churning.

Without hesitation, he said, "We have decided to get into that business and want them in the package." When you are dealing with a horse trader, some things never change! I offered 600 acres of fee land around the refinery and a G-1 airplane as a trade, and suddenly Southland was not interested in the chemical business.[2]

This was a nice coup for me, and I had made both my management and Southland happy again, but the fact that we might operate another business on the refinery site raised other potential long-term problems that had to be defined in the contract. It proved to be worth the trouble, however. Ray's chemical group modernized the plants, which became very successful over the following years. If Dr. Hammer had hired Ray one month later, this change would never have happened. Timing, as always, is everything. I could see God's hand working on our behalf, but he wasn't finished.

* * *

The complexity of this deal went way beyond anything I had been involved in. Not only did we have to deal with the fifteen-year agreement for Southland to purchase our crude oil, but after the sale, Oxy would maintain ownership of a natural gas liquids plant in the middle of the refinery that would be operated by personnel who would begin to work for Southland at the signing of the stock purchase agreement. Our natural gas liquids plant would continue to furnish raw materials to their refinery. We also furnished product from the same plant to outside sources. We would own the plant, but Southland would operate it. You can imagine the contracts necessary to define that relationship!

Suffice it to say, the final agreement at the time of closing involved some seventy-five exhibits and over twenty contracts. In a single stack, all the documents would measure somewhere between 3.5 to 4 feet in height. I had the great advantage of having one very special lawyer at Oxy who carried with him, wherever he went, the full closing agreement. I think that his right arm grew about three inches during the six months we worked on the contract. He knew every article, exhibit, and contract, and his expertise in such matters served Oxy well since a major part of their business was buying and selling things. It was the nature and complexity of all these documents, however, that brought about another confrontation with Sam and put my survival at Oxy in question.

On Wednesday, before the stock purchase agreement was to be signed on Thursday, I had a heart-to-heart talk with all our attorneys. They consisted of two outside legal firms and Oxy's inside corporate counsel. We discussed where we were in the finalization of all exhibits and contracts to be attached to the stock purchase agreement, and the news was not good. Only 10 percent of the documents were completed. The consensus was that Southland was stalling the completion of the documents so that some issues could be further negotiated after the signing. This was certainly not in Oxy's favor. We already had too many issues that would be long-standing, difficult problems for many years in the future.

I met with Sam that night for a late dinner. It proved to be interesting, if not the cause of indigestion for both of us. We were scheduled to sign the agreement in the Southland offices in Dallas the next day, complete with CEOs, board members, and television coverage. It was going to be a big affair. Just as Sam was about to take his first bite, I said, "Sam, you guys are slow playing us on the documents. We are not going to sign tomorrow. We will sign when all of the documents are complete, whenever that is."

Sam looked like he was going to have a stroke. "Have you talked to Dr. Hammer about this?"

"No, but I plan on calling him this evening." Remember, this was before cell phones and e-mail.

Sam got up, went to the pay phone in the restaurant, and called John Thompson. When he came back, he was red as a beet. "John doesn't care if the deal is ever signed."

It was now my turn. I walked over to the pay phone and called Bob Abboud instead of Dr. Hammer. What a chicken I was! When I told Bob the ultimatum I had just issued to Sam, he immediately told me to call him in the doctor's office. When I called, the doctor exploded "What do you mean we are not signing tomorrow?"

I said that it was not in our best interest to sign until all the documents were completed. He asked why we did not go ahead and sign, then work out the details later. I told him that was exactly what they wanted us to do. He said he did not like it, and then he hung up on me. This was not exactly a great situation to be in, especially for someone who had been with Oxy less than a year, was in the process of eliminating his position, and had no idea where he stood in future plans!

Then something miraculous happened. When Sam and I returned to Southland's attorneys' office about 10:00 p.m. that night, there were more lawyers working than I had seen in four months. I don't know how long they stayed, but I can tell you we signed the final stock purchase agreement on Friday at noon in Dallas with almost every document in its final form. At the reception following, neither Dr. Hammer nor John Thompson spoke to me; however, I drew consolation from knowing I had done the right thing, and my future was in God's hands, not theirs.

* * *

After the signing of the stock purchase agreement, we headed toward the final closing of the deal. A serious potential setback took place just before the day of the signing, one that could have blown the whole Oxy-Southland deal. We had agreed to schedule the signing of the stock purchase agreement according to the completion of the coker project at the Lake Charles refinery, a critical aspect of the deal for Southland. A couple of days before our final closing, one of the key people at Lake Charles called and informed me that during the pressure testing of the coker, something went awry and it imploded.

For a moment, I thought this must be some kind of sick joke. Then it suddenly dawned on me that the person on the other end of the line was not laughing. To give you an idea of how serious this was, the coker vessel was the major part of a $300 million project being finalized at the refinery, and it would take another nine months to get a new coker delivered, in place, and tested.

I knew I had to call John Thompson, and I learned a lot about the man in one short conversation. I figured there was a good chance he would kill the deal, as most would. Instead, after I told him what had happened, he said that we would continue with the deal and manage the ramifications of the accident later, when we understood the impact more fully. With this response, we went forward to a closing in late August of 1983.

Of course, the coker accident became a major item in the future since Southland's business at the refinery would be greatly impaired until the coker operation was fully restored. The challenge was determining how much Southland lost because the coker had not been operational at the closing of the deal. Interestingly enough, negotiations went smoother and an agreement was reached much quicker than I expected. Compared to some of the other conditions of the stock purchase agreement, which carried on years after we signed the deal, this was a piece of cake.

The party at the final closing was held in Dallas. All of the principle participants in this six-month process were there, and Sam and I were recognized for what we had accomplished. Most people did not understand the amount of work involved and the give-and-take required to arrive at such a deal and, for Sam and me, how much fun we had doing it. During the closing dinner, Dr. Hammer said a few words about how pleased he was and made reference to the fact that for years to come, Southland would continue to purchase oil at a favorable price from Oxy. Someone from Southland turned to me and said, "I told you that's what he said."

My retort was "That is not what he meant."

The manner by which we priced our sales of oil to Southland under the newly closed sale would be a thorn in our side for many years and the cause of numerous legal actions. At the time of the sale, the basis for pricing crude oil had to do with posted prices. In a variety of US locations, the companies or their brokers posted the price at which they would acquire crude oil for their refineries. These prices would vary to some degree based on the needs of the companies. In other words, a company that needed oil more than others would pay more than one that needed less. There was never much difference in price per barrel until you brought large volumes into play.

With regard to the Oxy-Southland deal that went into effect in 1983, we would look at the posted prices in the area, determine what the average price was, and that was what we used. This also ensured the royalty owners, or the owners of the mineral rights on the land where the oil was drilled, a royalty on the same basis as before our agreement. This method would pass legal scrutiny as it was the only basis by which all domestic sales were made in the country at that time. However, over the next three or four years, the way in which oil was priced changed dramatically. Many began to base their price on the general market or the price based on supply and demand in various parts of the country or in the world. This is called spot pricing. Since the spot market continually fluctuated, a constant dialogue between Southland and Oxy was required to agree to the price for crude oil sales. They wanted it low and we wanted it high.

The change from posted pricing to spot pricing happened gradually, which complicated matters even more. The brokers continued to post prices even after spot pricing became commonplace, and there was hardly a time in the fifteen years of our contract with Southland that the posted prices and the spot pricing agreed. There also was no consistency as to the difference. One day, one was high and the other low, and the next day, they would reverse positions. Why posted prices were even still available after spot pricing became commonplace has always been a mystery to me.

The difficulty of setting prices for our oil also complicated the calculation of royalties we paid to the royalty owners. After years had passed, an attorney alleged that royalty owners had been cheated. It was his contention that the contract signed in 1983 was worded in such a way as to pay less to the royalty owners than they were due. To think we knew that the pricing mechanism would change during the fifteen years of our contract gave us credit for being much smarter than we really were!

The fact that we had fought really hard to avoid giving any discount to Southland on the price of crude indicates we were always seeking the highest price we could get, which was in our royalty owners' best interest as well as our own.

I spent twelve hours in a deposition over this issue. The lawyer basically asked the same question over and over, but he worded it a little bit differently each time. The idea was to get me to say that the change in pricing happened because of something unfair we had embedded in our agreement, and not something that happened throughout the whole industry in the natural course of events.

This was the only deposition I ever gave that was filmed, and my lawyer impressed upon me how important my body language was. Thanks to Oliver Howard, I did reasonably well. Whenever he saw that I was about to lose my temper, he made some kind of movement or outburst to remind me to keep my cool and allow him to reveal how irritated he was with the line of questioning.

I learned from this experience that you should never make an agreement in which every minute detail and contingency of the transaction is not covered as best you can anticipate. What you do not spell out in writing always has the potential to put you in a courtroom years later, trying to remember what you did and said and why. You can also find yourself at the mercy of having someone else determine what is fair instead of the parties involved.

* * *

The time spent with Southland was not only very educational, but also provided the opportunity to get to know some wonderful people. Although I haven't seen Sam Susser in years, my time with him was both productive and fun. He was a worthy opponent, and I very much appreciated our sparring sessions. The Thompson family gave me an offer to work for them, and they were so nice and successful that I considered it, especially as I pondered what I would be doing after my obligatory year of the five-year contract with Oxy.

It was interesting that the one-year term of my employment contract with Oxy and the final closing of the Southland-CITGO deal both occurred on the same date in August of 1983. It was still not clear how I fit into Oxy's plans. After all, I had upset the doctor by delaying the signing of the stock purchase agreement. As I thought about what other opportunities God might have for me, I got a phone call from Bob Abboud. He invited me to have dinner with him the following evening in Los Angeles.

To be truthful, I was not worried. If he was going to fire me, he certainly would not do it over dinner. During the dinner, Bob said they wanted me to stay and take over the domestic operation of Oxy. That would include the operations of both Cities and Oxy. I was pleased to accept his offer. I would be the chairman and CEO of Cities Service, which by that time had become the domestic operation for Occidental Petroleum based in Tulsa.

The next thing Bob brought up floored me. He indicated Oxy wanted to buy out my contract and write me a new one. My first thought was *Why would they do that?* He asked me to tell him what I wanted for a payout on the contract. I had no idea what value to put on my contract and had never thought about it, so I told him I would think about it as we ate.

By the time we were well into dinner, I was able to give Bob some idea what I thought it was worth, and we agreed to a figure. Then he offered me a new contract with Oxy that was considerably more than I was making under my present contract! I was overwhelmed and could hardly wait to tell Clydella. Imagine, I had the job I wanted, for more money than I ever dreamed I would make, and we would stay in Tulsa.

Not everyone was as happy as I was about my new job, however. The employees of the acquiring company (in this case Oxy) usually don't expect their new boss to be promoted from the acquired company (in this case Cities). They expect the most important jobs to be filled from their own pool of employees. To say that some Oxy personnel were not pleased with my appointment is an understatement. Nevertheless, I was not offended because I understood how I would have felt if our situations had been reversed. Knowing that allowed me to proceed with few encumbrances, and there was a lot to do.

By the time we completed the CITGO sale, we had sold close to $2 billion dollars of assets, but it was still far short of the goal. Our goal had been $3 billion, which would repay the debt Oxy incurred to purchase Cities Service. We also had hoped the price of oil would increase enough to provide the additional cash flow to pay down the remaining balance of the debt, but it didn't. In fact, the price of oil was under attack, and by 1986, it took a free fall that was scary.

It is unfortunate that almost the only way to create more cash in the ensuing years was by reducing costs, i.e., reducing the size of the organization. Furthermore, when two companies in the same business combine, there are employees in each company who do the same job and one of them has to be eliminated. Every time I had to lay off anyone, it upset me, and it still bothers me to this day. I prayed that the Lord would give me the wisdom to do this in a way that recognized and minimized the terrible impact on the families involved. When oil prices dropped drastically, layoffs were going to happen, whether I did it or someone else did. So I tried to do it with the utmost care and concern.

God had brought me upstream and I was grateful, but I also realized that with each promotion, the challenges were greater, and because of that, good relationships were often more difficult to maintain. As the responsibilities and pressures, and heartbreak at letting people go increased, I remembered what Jesus said, "To whom much is given, from him much will be required" (Luke 12:48, NKJV). That verse had become a reality for me.

EXPANSION OF MIND AND HEART

In 1983, I was chairman and president of Cities, the new domestic company of Oxy, and Clydella and I were empty nesters. Scott was in the MBA program at Texas A&M, and Steve and Stuart were at Oklahoma State, so we were pretty much free to travel to wherever I might have to go. I said "pretty much" because Clydella had been a full-time volunteer since we arrived back in Tulsa in 1977. She stayed as busy as I did and often had to stay home because of her obligations.

One night, I got a call from Dr. Hammer. He told me that his grandson, Michael, was an MBA graduate from Columbia and needed to learn something about the oil and gas business. He wanted to know if I would see that he got some firsthand experience. I never knew whether that was a question or an order.

About a month later, Michael showed up in my office. He looked like George Hamilton, a bronze statue raised in the California sunshine. As I remember, he had a mustache and looked like he had stepped out of a Hollywood movie. He was personable, but he seemed less than interested in what his grandfather wanted him to do. I arranged for him to go to Midland, Texas, Oklahoma City, and Houston. It was no surprise that all of these places together paled next to the excitement of Los Angeles. The six months did not go fast enough for him!

Early in 1984, I got another call from Dr. Hammer. He read me a letter from Michael that basically said that a girl had changed his entire life. Leaving his history of little to no commitment to the women in his life, he had become serious about someone he wanted his grandfather to meet, as soon as possible. The girl's name was Dru Mobley, and Dr. Hammer asked me if I knew her father, Doug, who evidently lived in Tulsa. I responded that I had never heard of him. He asked me to find out what I could about Doug before he met Dru, and I said I would.

I called a handful of people and got no information until I talked to George Nolley, an old friend and a board member of both Cities and Oxy. He said he had heard of Doug, who was a businessman, as well as a Christian evangelist, but that was all he knew. Next, I called my friend Bob Nash, who served on the board of the ORU Titan Club with me. He gave me the full scoop on the man.

Doug Mobley had been a successful residential housing developer, and his partner was Oral Roberts's son-in-law, Marshall Nash. After Marshall and his wife Rebecca were tragically killed in an airplane crash, Doug began his evangelistic ministry on a full-time basis, later deciding to combine his business with his ministry.

I asked Bob to arrange a breakfast meeting with Doug, and he did. Our conversation lasted over three hours! Afterward, I informed the doctor that Doug was a man of high character and someone I wanted to know better. Fortunately, our friendship grew through the years, and Michael and Dru got married before the end of 1985.

Before Michael could marry Dru, however, he had to become more familiar with Doug and his ministry than he ever bargained for. Doug was a born-again believer in Jesus Christ, and if you were going to marry into his family, you needed to know Jesus as your personal Lord and Savior. Before the marriage, Michael gave his life to Jesus, and Doug's godly influence would be felt throughout the Hammer family in the years to come.

* * *

Merging the domestic units of Cities and Oxy in 1983 was not difficult, since we seemed to operate in different areas of the United States. The hard thing for me was learning the corporate culture of Oxy, which was remarkably different from Cities's. Cities Service Company had been very traditional compared to Occidental Petroleum, which really became a company when Dr. Hammer became involved in the early 1960s. At that time, I think Oxy had three employees. It was his audacity to compete with the big players in our industry that put Oxy in a position of buying Cities, a much bigger company.

Just prior to acquiring Cities, Oxy had bought IBP, a large commercial processor of beef and pork. It was through this transaction that a man named David Murdock acquired a large stock interest in Oxy and was seated on the board. When I entered the scene as head of Oxy's domestic upstream business, I began the next major phase of my MBA. This course would be all about internal corporate power plays. It became apparent early on that there were two factions operating within Oxy, and each had the intention of seeing the other go away.

One faction was led by Dr. Hammer and the other was led by David Murdock. Murdock became an outspoken critic of Dr. Hammer and his activities. Amazingly, the president of Oxy seemed to be a covert member of the Murdock group. Although he tried to keep his position quiet, it was evident to those who were really listening. The first question in my mind was *Why would the doctor put up with this?*

The truth was that the doctor was never fearful. He knew he was in control, and I am not certain he didn't enjoy what was going on. If they thought he was not aware of what they were doing, they were not very smart! One group was always trying to trump the other. These maneuvers may have entertained Dr. Hammer, but they made it difficult for those of us who were running operations.

Nothing like this was allowed at Cities, and so the politics were new to me, but early on, I developed a strategy to deal with it. If the president's group called and asked some important question, I would always find a way to give the doctor's group the same answer, even if the question was not on their agenda. I did not, however, pass along any information from the doctor's group to the president's group. My loyalty was to the man in charge, not those who were operating under a different agenda.

While this was a very unproductive situation, it was a great lesson in the politics of large corporations. Over the years, I have also learned that it applies to smaller groups and other kinds of companies, including nonprofits. It should not be surprising that politics, or turf wars as we call it, are something created by humans and have little to do with the organizational structure or the policies of that structure. It was only a matter of time before the doctor would tire of this game and make a move to correct a bad situation.

At the same time this was going on, I settled into the job of running the domestic upstream operation. The only significant addition of property was from the Oxy California operation. Much of the initial domestic production that put Oxy in business was from the heavy oil or low gravity oil plays in that area.[3] They also had taken a few blocks in the offshore California trend, in this case the Santa Maria basin.[4,5] Chevron had a large discovery in the trend, and Oxy was looking to drill there also. Unfortunately, the well that was drilled on the Oxy block tested for oil that was barely in the double-digit gravity range, meaning it was very thick, viscous, and hard to produce.

The biggest problem in offshore drilling in California was always whether the state government was going to issue a permit to let you develop what you found. Our problem was even more complicated because ten-degree gravity oil is not very desirable, especially in an offshore setting. Still, it appeared that under our block, there might be as much as one hundred million barrels, blocks, or cubes—however ten-degree oil comes out.

By the time I arrived, we had agreed with our partners to move forward with the permit process and to order an offshore platform to produce, or try to produce, the block. The former was a waste of time and the latter was money poorly spent. While the platform was being built in Korea, we attempted to make some headway in the permit process. However, very early on, I realized we would never get the permit in time to receive the platform. We needed to take action quickly to bring some solvency to the deal.

Shell was a partner in this venture and represented much more staying power than we had or had wanted. I traveled to Houston and was able to sell our interest and the operatorship to Shell for what we had invested in the prospect. Some people thought I was crazy, but in the next two years, Shell was never able to get a permit for the development of the block, and eventually, the partnership had to write off the total cost as a loss, which was in the order of $400 million. There has been no development in this area since that time.

As 1984 was closing, the doctor did tire of the antics of the rival inside group. In a speedy move, Oxy bought back the shares owned by David Murdock and eliminated him from the board. I got a call to come to a Saturday morning meeting at Dr. Hammer's house in Los Angeles. I had no idea what to expect. When I got there, I noticed that the president of Oxy was the only member of the operating team who was absent. Dr. Hammer announced that Ray Irani was the new president of Oxy, and from that date on, we would report to him.

The doctor's solution was a blessing in two ways. First, it eliminated the covert atmosphere, and second, it put into place someone I had grown to respect in the short time I had known him. Ray brought a lot of good business sense to the chemical group and would do the same for the rest of Oxy. That meeting was very short, but the impact was long-lasting.

* * *

When Ray Irani had come to Oxy from Olin Chemical, he also brought along his right-hand man. It is common for a new person from another company to bring personnel they know they can trust. They need people with whom they can talk freely about all the issues. Ray brought Dale Laurance, who had the most unusual job I had ever seen in a corporation. He became the contact for all of the business heads to get information to and from Ray.

I believe Ray trusted me, but I never became someone he shared things with or even communicated with on a regular basis. During the many years I ran the largest business in Oxy, I probably had less than twenty-four hours of conversation with him altogether! The only exception to this protocol was the chemical group because Ray actually ran the business through the same people he had brought with him. But the rest of us communicated with him through Dale.

For several years, Dale never appeared on any organizational chart. While the organizational structure of Dr. Hammer was far from conventional, at least all the people had some place on the chart! But Dale was not listed, even though he was our main contact. Most people on the outside didn't know what he did. He was the invisible man who had prime access to the person in charge and more stroke than the rest of us put together.

Needless to say, it was not easy to get used to communicating with Ray through Dale. However, over time, I saw that what I said to Dale was exactly what Dale said to Ray, and any insecurity or suspicion I had about the arrangement disappeared. As soon as I knew I could trust him, Dale and I became the best of friends. We certainly did not always agree, but we found a way to share our differences of opinion that improved our response to difficult situations.

Dale and Ray are two of the smartest people I ever worked with, especially in their ability to get things done. Not only was Ray the only one of many presidents under Dr. Hammer who survived, but when the doctor died in 1990 and Ray took his place, he made sense of the mountain of difficulties he inherited. I am always thankful the Lord placed me in a position to assist Ray and Dale in running the company, before and after Dr. Hammer's death. With problems of all magnitudes, working with people who are wise and honest makes the difference.

* * *

The major challenges we had to deal with after the merger were too much debt and a market for oil that was going in the tank. When you have very little leeway to grow your business and no way to increase the price of your product, the only way to change the bottom line and survive is to reduce the cost of doing business. While the need to do this surfaced in 1984, the situation became acute in 1986, when the Saudis flooded the market with oil to try to bring some discipline to OPEC producers. Oil prices fell to something below $9 per barrel.

The economic environment in America and the oil industry in general had been very healthy, and there was a lot of growth up until 1982 We were dealing with a problem that seems to recur more frequently than not. When business is going well and there seems like no end to prosperity, plans expand to accommodate anticipated growth. This always involved people. Later when markets falter, prices go down, and costs rise, the end result is always the same. We faced a reduction in force, or downsizing or right sizing. What ever you want to call it, it was and is a miserable experience.

What we went through then is very similar to what is happening now as I write this book. Government cites economic recovery, but any increase in corporate performance has little to do with increased production, increased sales, or profit margins early on. The increase in profitability is due more to reductions in workforce, reductions that have taken place across all industries to reduce costs and improve income. When you can't increase sales or prices, your only option is to reduce the size of the organization, and that causes unemployment to rise. The federal government has never understood this because they have never had a reduction in work force!

As a result of all these factors, from 1984 to 1989, we were forced to reduce our workforce from about

5,000 people to about 1,600. Approximately 1,000 of those people were employees of assets we sold to other companies. These reductions were the most difficult tasks I had in my forty-year career. It was easy to justify that we had no other course of action and that if I did not do it, someone else would. Nevertheless, it was something I still find painful.

What made this action even more difficult was that I knew so many people in the organization. I had worked in every division of Cities Service but the chemical group. Therefore, the people I was terminating were those I had spent time with over the years. At least I had a clear objective that took my feelings out of the equation. The objective was to retain the best and most skilled workers, and I hope we were successful in doing that. No one was kept because of my friendship or former relationship with them. I assured management I would protect no one in the process, and I didn't want anyone else to either.

I looked at every list as the selection of people to be terminated was decided. It should never be anything other than a heartrending situation for anyone responsible for this undertaking, and it was for me. Personally, I made all these decisions covered in prayer that we would all do this correctly.

I was very fortunate to have two very close Christian friends that were running corporations and going through the same experience. Bob Parker, Jim Barnes, and I were always available to each other when we needed reinforcement from someone in the same boat. They still are very special to me.

* * *

With 1986 came several other events of great import. First, Oxy purchased Mid-Con Corporation, a primarily gas pipeline company with oil and gas production in a couple of subsidiaries. Oxy had been searching for such a company. Mid-Con had been put into play through a hostile offer that allowed Oxy to become a white knight.

As we were flying to Chicago to make Mid-Con an offer, Ray was schooling Dr. Hammer on how to negotiate the deal. He suggested we should first offer them $2 billion and then, if conditions required, we would go to $2.2 billion. The doctor took all this in as Ray repeated the strategy more times than necessary. At the airport, Dr. Hammer got in the car with Ray and Cliff Davis, the CEO of Mid-Con. Dale and I got into another car. By the time we got to the Mid-Con offices, Dr. Hammer had already done the deal at the higher price. He was a dealmaker, not a negotiator!

The Mid-Con purchase gave Oxy a large pipeline system in the United States, which Dr. Hammer thought would enable us to raise the price on some of the old gas contracts. Cities had entered into these contracts in the early days of gas production, and some were drawn up as far back as the 1930s. At that time, gas had no value and was normally flared or burned on site. Back then, the first guy with Cities who signed a gas contract for 15 cents per MCF (million cubic feet) may have been the biggest hero in company history; however, a big change was taking place that these old contracts had not foreseen. The potential value of natural gas to the overall energy supply in the United States was understood by more people. Unfortunately, the old contracts we had with purchasers of our oil and gas set the price of natural gas at the old contract value, and they were lifetime contracts. By the time we acquired Mid-Con, natural gas was up to about $3 MCF. If we sold our gas for 15 cents MCF, we would be making next to nothing and wasting a very valuable energy source. Most oil companies faced the same problem.

All of these disputes were eventually run through the courts as oil and gas companies tried to abrogate their contracts, but all decisions were in favor of the purchasers because the courts could only uphold the contracts, even though they were based on an outdated value for natural gas. A contract could not be broken unless both parties agreed, and of course, the purchaser was going to stick to the lower price!

The only way we could get out of these outdated, unprofitable contracts was to buy them out. The purchasers made a lot of money on this deal, but at least we were now free to negotiate new contracts with pricing that would reflect the current value of natural gas. Our need to settle these old contracts caused the value of the Mid-Con purchase to be less than we thought the company was worth, and it would take a while for this mistake to be corrected on the balance sheet of Oxy.

* * *

In the early part of 1986, I received a call that Ray Irani was going to be coming to Tulsa and wanted to have lunch with me. Ray had never been to Tulsa, and I had no idea what he wanted to discuss. As we ate, Ray informed me that he wanted to consolidate the domestic and international business, and he wanted me to be the chairman and CEO of the combined operations, Occidental Oil and Gas Corporation. I was dumbfounded. The international organization was still upset that I had been given the domestic business! Although four years had passed, I knew they would really be angry about this move.

I carefully considered what my answer should be. Ray and I had few private conversations, so we knew very little of each other except from a business standpoint. The respect was there, but there was no familiarity to guide me. I decided what my response should be.

"Ray, I am a born-again Christian, and as best I can, I try to run my business with those principles in mind. Now I realize you may not have known this when you decided to offer me this position, so if it makes a difference to you, feel free to change your mind. I will find something else to do."

He thought for a minute and said, "That's not a problem to me."

With this understanding, I took on the responsibility of running Occidental Oil and Gas Corporation, Oxy's worldwide oil and gas business. Not long after that, I received another interesting offer. One of the ex–board members of Southland Corporation, Elvis Mason, who was the previous chairman of the First National Bank of Dallas, had formed a company named Mason-Best. They had purchased a company, Tracor, that provided materials for the Defense Department and were in the early stages of putting together an oil and gas company. Ralph Bailey, who had been the CEO of Conoco, was the CEO of the new company. As you remember, I had not been impressed with the way Ralph and Conoco had conducted themselves in 1981 when they simultaneously negotiated with Cities and Seagram for a solution to their problem.

Elvis asked me to come to Dallas and have lunch, giving me no indication why. When I arrived, he was there with Ralph. They asked me to come to work for them and be Ralph's successor after a few years. I thought about it during our conversation, but my answer was not hard to find. I told them I had been given a new responsibility with Oxy and would honor the commitment I had made to Ray Irani. Moreover, there were things that needed to be done at Oxy, and I would not consider going anywhere else until those issues had been resolved. They asked how long that would take, and I said at least a year. I was convinced I had put an end to those discussions.

About a year later, I got another call from Elvis. He wanted to know how things had been going over the last year. After a few preliminaries, he asked if I was now in a position to consider his offer, which was still open. I agreed that the next time I was in Dallas I would come to see him. As always, I prayed I would get some kind of divine nudge as to what I should do before then.

A month or so later, I was in Dallas and visited again with Elvis and Ralph. They filled in more of the details of what they were doing and how I would fit into their vision for the future. Then I said, "My business life is directed by God, and I am only comfortable knowing he has placed me where I'm supposed to be. So I will pray about it and talk with my wife and then get back to you." They both looked at me like I was speaking another language. I returned to Tulsa and waited for some indication as to what I should do.

It should not be amazing, but it always is when God answers so clearly and sometimes so supernaturally that there is no doubt about the course of action you should take. Bob Nash called one evening to say that Bruce Olson was in town and was speaking at our church the next day.

Bruce is a very special person and friend. At the age of seventeen, he went to South America as a missionary to the indigenous tribes of Colombia and Venezuela. As of this writing, he has been there for almost fifty years and has become an icon in Colombia. He has been the conduit God has used to convert almost the total population of the indigenous tribes to Christianity, many times to his peril. He has been kidnapped twice by the guerillas, once for a period of nine months. Before he was released, he was put before a firing squad and was sure he was going to see Jesus in heaven momentarily. He was relieved when the bullets fired were blanks, and they let him go.

Since I had overseen South American operations for Cities and Oxy had a very large presence in Colombia, over the years I had been able to spend time with Bruce in Bogota and Bucaramanga during my travels there. Oxy had discovered a billion-barrel oil field in Colombia in the mid-1980s. The field was near the Venezuela border, which meant the oil would have to travel by pipeline from the field to a terminal on the coast of Colombia. The pipeline was laid over the Andes Mountains to reach a terminal at the Port of Covenas, Colombia, where the oil would be loaded onto tankers and delivered to the market.

Once the field was developed, the guerillas were constantly trying to stop the flow of the oil to the market. Over the years of producing more than one billion barrels, I would estimate that the pipeline was blown up close to a thousand times. Ecopetrol, the government oil company, operated the pipeline and became expert in repairing it, certainly not by desire but out of necessity.

During this time, Bruce Olson was captured for the second time by the guerillas. The first time was very short. The second time, he was in captivity for nine months. During his captivity, the guerillas attacked our terminal in Covenas. The damage they did was significant, but not catastrophic.

What we found out later was that when the guerillas had planned the raid at Covenas, Bruce was in captivity and able to overhear their conversations. After his release, he immediately told me and the Colombian government what the guerillas were planning. He was not aware that the raid had already taken place. I flew Bruce to Bakersfield to debrief our security people regarding all he knew about how the guerillas operated and any plans they had for the future. He was probably better informed about what was happening in Colombia than anyone in our group.

Bruce happened to be in Tulsa, and that was purely an "accident." He had been scheduled to do an interview on television in New York before returning to Colombia, but at the last minute, his spot on the program was cancelled. Instead, he flew to Tulsa where a large base of his supporters lived. As you may know, missionaries must come home periodically to report their progress and raise funds to continue their work abroad.

As Bruce was talking that day at our church, he made a strong point that some people are put in high positions to be able to support God's work in the area where they are involved, and we had been especially able to do exactly that for Bruce and his people in Colombia. The moment he said that, I saw a bright light cover his head, and at that moment, I knew for certain I was supposed to remain at Oxy for that very reason.

I called Elvis the next day to explain what had happened and that I would not be accepting his offer. Again, he did not seem to understand why, but he did understand my answer. I never had another occasion to think about going somewhere else.

* * *

During the early part of 1988, I made a trip to Scotland to visit the offices in Aberdeen as well as two platforms in the North Sea. One of those was the Piper Platform, which was producing about 100,000 bpd (barrels per day) and had been for some years. The trip was an eye-opener to me. While I had been on many platforms in the Gulf where the platforms were built to withstand hurricane winds and waves of twenty-five feet, it was my first time in the North Sea, where they built the platforms to withstand hundred-foot waves. Wind is much easier to withstand than water!

In July of that year, I received a call one night that the Piper Platform had exploded and was burning. Rescue crews were trying to get to the remains of the platform, but the heat was too intense. The first thing I thought of was all the people I had met and watched as they worked on that platform. By early morning in the North Sea, we learned that 167 of the 223 people on the platform did not survive. All those who were rescued were seriously injured. We were devastated.

Dr. Hammer traveled to Scotland and met with British Prime Minister Margaret Thatcher to discuss what should take place as a result of the accident. She formed a commission that would meet for more than a year to investigate what happened and what actions were necessary to prevent a further tragedy. The commission found that the accident was caused by human error, which was compounded by original design deficiencies used specifically for production systems in the North Sea.

The changes proposed by the commission were put in place, and we did everything we could to take care of the families of both the dead and the living. The legal department of Oxy revealed great compassion as they dealt with this tragic situation. Settlements that were generous considering the Scottish laws at the time were made with all but one of the families, which I believe may have been settled through a lawsuit filed in Houston.

I love lawyers, but not all of them! It was amazing to me that in less than forty-eight hours of the accident, there were Houston attorneys on the ground in Scotland to try and establish jurisdiction in Texas. Some people have no qualms about propriety when money is involved. This kind of action made me even more proud of the way our own attorneys handled all but one of the settlements.

Events like the North Sea tragedy were something you never want to be part of, but sometimes, doing business means implied risks, risks that could possibly lead to the loss of human life. Other risks led to layoffs. But in all these difficult times, God was always there. He saw me through it, and as I followed his instructions, my life changed for the better in ways I never could have imagined. He showed me that in difficult times, in seeking him for solutions or praying for sheer staying power, my mind opened to new possibilities and my heart expanded in compassion for others.

* * *

One of the things you are afforded in corporate leadership is a platform to express who you are and what you believe. Some would say you need to be discreet in availing yourself of that privilege. What they are really saying is, "Try not to offend anyone else's belief." I agree with that as long as it doesn't require me to compromise what I believe.

Some people decide not to use the platform they have been given. They fear their transparency may lead to difficulties with people in the future. Fortunately, I was never restrained by such feelings, and in late 1985, reviewing the difficult times we had gone through, were still going through and would go through for years to come, I decided to issue a brief summary of the year's events and combine my report with a Christmas message.

That first year, I read it over the PA system in our Tulsa building, but I did not send a written form of the message to people outside of Tulsa. Some would later say the message was not appropriate because it was overtly Christian. Since the basis for the season is the birth of Jesus Christ, I always want to say, "Duh." I continued giving a Christmas message every year, and before I retired the first time, I was sending the message to all the oil and gas employees around the world. When I came out of retirement in 1995 for four years, I issued the messages again. During that time, I was in Canada, and I'm almost certain none of those employees had ever received anything like that from a CEO!

The Christmas letter was done for two purposes: to recap what had gone on in the company in the past year and to put what had taken place in the proper perspective, considering the special season celebrating God's greatest gift to mankind. Following are my favorite excerpts from those messages over the years:

> 1985: As a Christian, Christmas is so special to me. The birth of Christ in our religion

represents God's gift to a world in need of a solution to the problems of the time. Christians believe that the solutions Jesus offered during His life are very applicable to the current times and are made more apparent during the Christmas season.

1986: But one time each year, we are brought to the reality of the manger and, once again, have to decide whether that Life and the significance it represents was no different than any other life, or whether it represents the only true significance, where we can find stability and meaning in our beliefs, and principles, and the fundamentals important in our corporate and personal lives.

1987: Christmas reminds us of God's gift to an unbelieving world, the gift of His Son. It reminds us of His life and the characteristics of that Life that were so special and so distinct and so different from many of the emotions and desires of today. It causes us to wonder what was, and is, different about Jesus. What is the special ingredient that was born in Bethlehem and lives on today, and can change each of our lives, our nation, even the world.

1988: Don't let this season, a season that is so founded in God's love for all of us, pass by without having told each one of those close to you that you love them and about the special part they play in your life. Open your heart to those around you who are less fortunate and who can be blessed by your concern for them in whatever way you choose to register that concern. The manner in which you celebrate this season, the manner in which your attitude conveys an understanding of the season, is a direct reflection to others as to how well you understand the meaning of, "For God so loved the world."

1989: The answer to all our confusion in the world and with our personal lives is so simple as the birth of a Child some 2,000 years ago, and in the meaning and hope that He brought to a world in need. May this Christmas be special to you and your family. May you celebrate it in a manner consistent with the love and feeling so wrapped up in the phrase, "For God so loved the world."

1990: Christmas is a season that celebrates the way. In my church, Christmas is God's gift of His Son. Christmas is love: love of God, love of family, love of each other, and love of country. Christmas is giving: giving of presents is the traditional way we use to celebrate. More meaningful than material gifts is the giving of ourselves to our families. Even more meaningful is the giving of ourselves to others who, during the season, have no one with whom to share Christmas. Giving to others of ourselves and whatever we can share carries with it the highest of rewards. To paraphrase, "In that you did this to others, you did it also unto Me."

1991: Let each of us decide during this Christmas season that we will respond to others in a way that would please God. There is no other meaningful way for Him to be revealed to others than through each of us.

1992: (This was my last message before I retired the first time.) Somehow it seems that any time the going gets tough, it becomes easier to abandon principle, ethics, and the simple decisions of right and wrong. Maybe these historical building blocks around which this nation was created were not meant for this day and age. Maybe such things as human dignity and integrity have served their purpose and are to be replaced by thoughts and actions that focus on each of us individually, with little thought given to the collective sense. Hopefully none of us believe that. The focus of what we should believe as individuals and as we come together collectively was set many years ago. "And you shall love the Lord your God with all your heart, mind, soul, and strength, and love you neighbor as yourself."

1996: (This was my last Christmas in Canada after coming out of retirement in late 1995. I don't know why I missed 1995!) We sometimes search for the "spirit of Christmas" and never realize that we are the conduit through which God creates that spirit. It is how we respond to our family, how we respond to those around us who are less fortunate, and how we respond to the One "from whom all blessings flow'" that makes the Christmas season special.

1997: (This was my first Christmas in Bakersfield, CA.) Please make this Christmas season a true reflection of God's love. Let's let our light so shine that others can make no mistake who we are and what we stand for. Economic environments are fickle. Organizations are dynamic, always changing. That will be no different in 1998 than in previous years. But the values on which a significant life is based never change. They are truly like God the same yesterday, today, and tomorrow.

1998: (This would be the last of my messages, since I retired again in early 1999.) In the Christian world, Christmas celebrates the birth of the Christ Child. It recalls for us the most celebrated and remembered person who was ever born. His life has impacted the world as no other and continues to do so today. For we who are Christians, a day does not go by that we are not influenced in our daily life and decisions by His presence. And most especially during this season, we are challenged by the example He set in serving those around Him who needed support during difficult times. To define what this means for us who follow, the Bible says, "To the extent that you have fed, clothed, and sheltered these, you have done it to Me." Pretty simple to understand.

I was gratified to receive some good responses like the following memo from an employee at Oxy:

I wanted to write a brief note on your Christmas message to the staff of the Company. Your speech was the subject of much debate throughout the evening. Some people I talked to wondered about the appropriateness of your speech. I thought it was very good. I think that we in North America are always too ready to sanitize everything we say for fear of offending anyone that we end up with no meaning at all. People forget that it is a Christmas Party not a Winter or End of Year party. Our culture preaches tolerance of other religions and traditions, yet we keep our own Christianity under wraps and hidden away. We forget that good Christian people built this continent up from wilderness in only 300 years. We should be proud of our faith; it made us what we are today.

It was never my intention to be dogmatic or abusive. It was just to be Dave. I always hope that I am what I say I am. It is only with the power of the Holy Spirit that I have any chance to do that. I very much miss that special opportunity I was given to lift the name of my Lord and Savior to people in my company.

THE END OF AN ERA

A surprise came in 1987 when I was elected to the board of Occidental Petroleum. It was especially a surprise to those who still had not accepted the fact that I had moved past them in the structure of Oxy. For me, being on the board was an incredible education, definitely one of the most meaningful of my MBA courses.

I was fifty-three, and this group of interesting and successful people, most who had been with the doctor for many years, included five members over the age of eighty. Dr. Hammer was eighty-nine himself. Some people would question the effectiveness of men that age, but after my association with this group, I never will.

John Kluge was the founder and CEO of Metromedia and very actively and successfully ran that business. Louis Nizer was still one of the best attorneys in the country, although his eyesight was failing. He had written at least ten books and was a capable screenwriter. He also continued to give briefs in front of the Supreme Court. Since he could not see to read his briefs, he would memorize his presentation. People would travel from around the country to hear him deliver a brief at the Supreme Court.

I mentioned George Nolley earlier. George and a friend, Walter Davis, had put together the Permian Corporation early in his career, which was eventually sold to Oxy. He also had been a long-term director of

Cities Service. He had become a director of Oxy in 1983 and had remained very active for almost twenty years.

Morrie Moss was a very humble man from Memphis. He would not seem very impressive if you did not know him or of him. While he was starting to have physical problems when I joined the board, his mind was sharp and his humor even more so. He wrote a book titled *The Importance of Unimportance*, which says a lot right there. You only need to check out the many chairs of businesses in Memphis, Vanderbilt, Tennessee, and Rhodes universities to recognize the impact Morrie had in his favorite state.

These were just some of the older people on the board at the time I became a director. I would learn much from these men as well as the other directors.

* * *

Although the oil field in Colombia was producing some 250,000 bpd, our oil and gas operations would struggle to stay healthy because of the debt incurred purchasing both Cities and Mid-Con. There were things that needed to be changed within Oxy to aid us in reducing the debt, but these changes would not be possible until the doctor passed away. No one was wishing for his demise, but we were preparing ourselves for the inevitable changing of the guard.

Ray Irani continued to work successfully with the doctor in a way that none of the many people who preceded him had ever done, and there had been many who preceded him. He also was very much aware of the changes necessary and was poised to see those take place when the time came.

One of the sticky problems at Oxy was that there were people who had come up the corporate ladder under Dr. Hammer, and they were not used to always doing things in a forthright and transparent way. If you asked them a question, they would answer only that question, often leaving out what Paul Harvey would call "the rest of the story." Therefore, you would not know what was really going on. I soon realized I had to find ways to discover the whole story. I'm sure this is prevalent in some other companies, but there is no question that it was the way things worked at Oxy.

When people tell you what you want to hear rather than the way things really are, you have to be discerning. This became a requirement for me to succeed in my job. I had to know when things needed to be pursued further. Listening only to the people who reported to me directly was not a good management style in the Oxy environment, or probably in any environment. I had to work out ways to hear from all levels of the organization, which caused me to develop skills many corporate leaders don't have.

On the other hand, there were many times when I was extremely gratified at the attitude and the work people at Oxy did. Our bottom line did not improve too much after 1986 when we had to lay off so many people. Every year thereafter, it seemed that the leaner we got, the leaner we needed to become, but 1989 was the worst of the worst. We had to reduce our workforce by about 1,000 people, which is when we were reduced to 1,600 employees.

The work required by my organization to do this in a manner that ensured the best and most qualified would remain was exceptional. We also established a job placement service internally that I believe was better than any similar organization on the outside. I had utmost respect for those involved in this process. They did a difficult job in circumstances no one wanted to face. By this time, I knew I had learned all I ever wanted to know about how to reduce a workforce.

Finally, during the latter part of 1989, it was very evident that Dr. Hammer was failing. He was ninety-one, but there were still things he wanted to do. The most important project had to do with his art collection, which had traveled the world. I have no idea what it cost the company to send it around the world on a yearly basis, but the people appreciated it. In China, they waited in line for days to view it. Art critics did not like the collection because it had been put together quickly and was used to further the doctor's purposes, but he never seemed affected by any critic. To say he moved to the beat of his own drum would be a gross understatement!

When we brought his art collection to the Philbrook Museum in Tulsa in 1984, it was a huge success and probably drew the most people of any collection viewed there. A funny thing happened, however. When the doctor arrived for the opening night in his private jet, I picked him up. The event that night was black tie, and for some reason, that day I had bought a tie-it-yourself tie and had become somewhat proficient in tying it. What I lacked was the confidence that it would stay together. With this concern, I put a pre-tied black tie in my pocket, just in case.

I took the doctor to the hotel first, so he could change clothes before going to the Philbrook. After waiting in the lobby for about five minutes, I got a call from him. He said, "Get my security guy, Ed Birch, to go to the store for me. I've forgotten a black tie."

I said, "Doctor, that is not a problem. I have an extra one in my pocket." I took it to his room. He never knew why I was carrying an extra tie, and I never told him.

In late 1989, as his health was deteriorating, Dr. Hammer asked the board to approve the construction of a museum to house his art. It would be located in the lower floors of the Oxy building in Los Angeles. He wanted his proposal to be approved by vote at that meeting so we could get started right away.

Those of us who were running operations were against the proposal. Our only reason was that we needed the money for projects with much greater possibilities. To the surprise of everyone, especially the doctor, Arthur Groman disagreed, indicating that many things would have to be done to do this legally. Dr. Hammer was almost speechless and obviously unhappy, to say the least. He was not used to having his orders questioned or delayed.

Arthur Groman had been a director of Oxy longer than anyone, and he was a well-known lawyer in Los Angeles. His judgment over the years had always been impeccable. The point he was making would prove my statement. He told the doctor that in order for this decision to be legal, a separate committee of independent directors would have to be appointed. They would then hire their own counsel to determine that spending the money for a museum would be beneficial to the shareholders. If it were not done in this manner, it would never stand the scrutiny it was sure to get.

As the discussion continued, the doctor got redder and redder. It was finally determined that this was the only way to proceed. Groman's instructions took some months to accomplish before we were ready to move forward with the project, and while the museum was being constructed, many select pieces of art were placed on the sixteenth floor of the Oxy building in Westwood. They lined the halls and covered the walls of the boardroom. I spent over a year at board meetings looking at a large painting by Gustave Moreau titled *Salome*, which was directly across from where I sat in the boardroom. It is the only painting I have ever studied for an extended time, and it became my favorite. We probably had paintings worth over $25 million in the boardroom alone. It was a real downer when the museum opened and we were looking at prints you could buy at a discount store!

✻ ✻ ✻

The museum opened in November 1990. It was evident this would be the final event on the doctor's long resume as he had to be carried in sitting in his chair. He died in the early part of December of that year. His private funeral was held not too far from the Occidental corporate office. There were six speakers, and one of them was Doug Mobley.

You may remember that Doug was the father of Dru Hammer, who was married to the doctor's only grandson, Michael. Even before the marriage of his daughter to Michael, Doug was praying about how he could bring the salvation message of Jesus Christ to the doctor. The opportunity came through Dru.

Michael and Dru had settled into a home in Los Angeles after their wedding, and Dru became very close to Victor Hammer, the doctor's younger brother. Victor was a very important part of the doctor's life, but was always in the background. He managed many things, especially the doctor's involvement in art and art galleries. As Dru and Victor became good friends, he sensed there was something different about her. He also had seen the change in Michael, and he was curious about it.

A few years later, Victor became very sick and spent some weeks in the hospital at UCLA. Finally, he was released and stayed at the Westwood Marquis Hotel in Los Angeles for a few days before leaving for Florida, where he spent some time every year. Doug and his wife Donna were in town, and Doug was nudged by the Holy Spirit to visit Victor. Since they were staying at the same hotel, they went right up to Victor's room. During the visit, Victor committed his life to Jesus. As Doug and Donna left the hotel that evening, Doug prayed that the Lord would give him confirmation of what had taken place.

That evening, Doug and Donna went out to eat with Michael and Dru, and Doug told them about leading Victor to the Lord. Of course, everyone was excited. When the four of them returned to Dru's home, Victor had left Dru a voice mail message, saying, "Your dad led me to the Lord this evening. I now know and have what you have." Needless to say, they were all thrilled.

The next day, Victor got on a plane for Florida, and less than forty-eight hours later, he went into a coma and died. His eternal life had been secured because Doug had followed the nudge of the Holy Spirit. God knew Victor was near the end, and he wanted to save him. He wants to save everyone.

More than anything else, this event created a bridge to Dr. Hammer that Doug would cross many times before the doctor died. On one of these occasions, a very humorous thing happened. Doug presented Dr. Hammer with a copy of the book *Mere Christianity* by C. S. Lewis. He felt that it could be essential to continuing discussions leading to his conversion. The doctor looked at it and said, "Yes, I remember when Clive wrote this." Neither Doug nor I had any idea what the *C* stood for in C. S. Lewis. So much for introducing the doctor to someone new!

I do not know how Doug approached his discussions with the doctor. He alone knows when the message got through and the doctor received Jesus as his Lord and Savior. I did not see a tremendous change in the doctor after he accepted Jesus, but that is true of a lot of us. Some of us are saved and immediately change our entire lifestyle, but some of us move more slowly. One thing I do know: it is not for us to monitor or become critical of how others are transformed through their new life in Jesus Christ.

One event would give credence to the eternal decision the doctor had made. A group of us were meeting at Doug's house in Tulsa while the doctor was on his deathbed in Los Angeles. During our prayer time, one of us prayed for Jesus to make himself known to the doctor during his final hours. I was getting ready to leave the meeting, so I knew it was 9:30 p.m., Tulsa time, when we prayed this prayer.

The doctor died that night, and after we arrived for his private funeral service, we visited with Rosa Maria Durazo, the doctor who had attended him in the last year of his life. We asked if there was anything unusual about his death. She reported that during the last few days, she had put a picture of Jesus on his bed stand. The evening he died, the doctor suddenly sat up in his bed, pointed at the picture of Jesus, and then passed. We asked what time it was. She said it was exactly 7:30 p.m., Los Angeles time. This was exactly the same time we finished praying in Tulsa. God does some wondrous things if we just listen and obey.

Doug related that story at the funeral service. Since Dr. Hammer was born of Jewish immigrants, the fact that he had received Jesus as his Messiah was received in many different ways at the gathering, especially since a rabbi was in charge of the service. No doubt a large percentage of the people, Jew and Gentile, were not believers, but they heard the Gospel that day.

* * *

Being around Dr. Hammer for eight years exposed me to some very interesting and famous people. The doctor always celebrated his birthday with a flare for the dramatic, and no one who was invited would miss it unless something catastrophic had happened to them. The first few years we attended these over-the-top events, Clydella and I would look at each other with an expression that said, "What are *we* doing here?" Although we eventually got used to being around so many powerful and well-known people, it was always foremost in our minds that it was only because God put us there.

Following are some highlights of the doctor's birthday galas.

1984: The doctor's eighty-sixth birthday gala would be the first Clydella and I attended. It was held at the Beverly Hilton Hotel, which at that time was owned by Merv Griffin. He was there, of course, along with Jane Morgan Wientraub, who sang "Happy Birthday." The entertainment was provided by one of the doctor's close friends, Mitslav Rostropovich, probably the most renowned cellist at the time. King Constantine of Greece was the center of attention.

1985: The doctor's eighty-seventh birthday gala was held at the Embassy Theater in Los Angeles. Rostropovich played with the Los Angeles Chamber Orchestra, Robert Merrill sang, and the ballets *Le Corsaire* and Fokine's *The Dying Swan* were performed. Attending were a baron with a name that is too long for me to pronounce or type, Michael Milken, Wayne Rodgers, Marvin Davis, the British ambassador to the

United States, Irving Stone, Sherry Lansing, Cary Grant, Patty Hearst, and many others.

Later in the year, Clydella and I had an additional thrill along these lines. Dr. Hammer and Prince Charles were establishing international colleges in different parts of the world. The doctor had started one in New Mexico and wanted to have a special event to raise money for the college. He convinced Prince Charles to come to Palm Beach, Florida, participate in a polo match and attend an evening gala. This was probably American society's event of the year, and we were invited!

It was surreal to go to the polo match and see Prince Charles play and then to spend the halftime on the field with Princess Diana, repairing divots made by the polo ponies. It was followed by a gala that evening that included Victor Borge, Bob Hope, Ted Turner, Ross Perot, Cornelius Vanderbilt Whitney, Robert Mosbacher, and many more foreign or wealthy dignitaries I did not know. Again, it was like an out-of-body experience.

1986: The doctor's eighty-eighth birthday gala was held at the Beverly Wilshire Hotel, Los Angeles. This event included Jimmy Stewart, Michael York, Merv Griffin, Charlton Heston, Alan Cranston, Gregory Peck, and Abigail Van Buren, better known as "Dear Abby." At every one of the parties, there were numerous local, state, and national politicians; this year Clydella's dinner partner was James Roosevelt, oldest son of President Franklin D. Roosevelt.

1987: The doctor's eighty-ninth birthday gala was held again at the Beverly Wilshire. Many of those attending were the same as the year before, so I will only add some of those who were new: Dinah Shore, Danny Thomas, Barbara Walters, Eva Gabor, and Helen Boehm. Clydella's partner was Cesar Romero, and Placido Domingo and Dinah Shore provided the entertainment.

This had been another very special party year. In February, Dr. Hammer and Lod Cook sponsored a charity event featuring the Duke and Duchess of York, the Duchess better known as "Fergie." Cook was the chairman and CEO of Atlantic-Richfield and was also a graduate of LSU. During his tenure as chairman of the LSU Foundation, he asked me to be on the board of the foundation, which I was for about six years. I sometimes think I have become a traitor to LSU because I have chosen to live in Oklahoma and am a great OSU fan. I like to think it is more a factor of geography. I love LSU, but I am never there.

The Fergie dinner was held at the Biltmore Hotel in Los Angeles. New faces to us were Roger Moore, Burt Bacharach, Joan Collins, George Hamilton, Arte Johnson, Buzz Aldrin, Lynda Bird Robb, and Walter Annenberg. Burt Bacharach and Carole Bayer Sager were the entertainment.

1988: The doctor's ninetieth birthday gala was held at the Watergate Hotel in Washington, DC. It would be a lavish weekend by any standard. Guests included the ambassador from the Soviet Union, Yuri Dubinin. Others were Lady Bird Johnson, Robert Schuller,

Sandra Day O'Connor, Randolph Hearst, Rhonda Fleming Mann, and the ambassadors of Bolivia, Venezuela, and Pakistan. The politicians and other dignitaries were too numerous to note.

The evening's entertainment was extraordinary. After dinner, we were all transported from the Watergate to the Kennedy Center for the Performing Arts. Those performing were cellist Rostropovich, dueling violinists Sir Yehudi Menuhin and Isaac Stern, Chinese pianist Yuhui Hong, and soprano Kiri Te Kanawa. The emcee was Merv Griffin. The performance lasted almost two hours and was a once-in-a-lifetime experience. Louis Nizer gave a very special recap of his relationship with the doctor, and his command of the English language amazed his hearers once again. The evening was complete when the doctor gave his birthday remarks.

1989: The doctor's ninety-first birthday gala was held at the Beverly Hills Hotel. Notable people attending were Helen Hayes and the McGuire Sisters, who were the entertainers for the evening, along with the Los Angeles Philharmonic. Our dinner partners were our close friends from Tulsa, George and Eunice Nolley; Sherry Lansing, the CEO of Paramount Pictures and her escort, Jack Haley Jr.; and Barbara Walters and her husband. To say that Barbara wanted to be at a table with more important people than the foursome from Tulsa is a gross understatement!

1990: The doctor's ninety-second and last birthday gala was held again at the Beverly Hills Hotel. It was apparent to those of us around him that he was struggling. The party was upbeat, but not the same magnitude as usual. The most notable person not mentioned before was the Archbishop of the Catholic Diocese of Los Angeles, Roger Mahony, who would be one of the speakers at the funeral later in the year.

* * *

As you can see, being around Armand Hammer was not all work. Many people believe the doctor was a communist and catered to the Russians. I never saw any sign of that, even given his history. He was born in Manhattan, and his parents were Russian Jewish immigrants, who were active socialists. As a young man, he traveled to Russia and started his business career there after a visit with Lenin. While he lived in Russia, he used this relationship for his own gain. After Lenin died, he left Russia because he never could accept Stalin. He knew the kind of person he was. At the time the doctor left Russia, he owned a pencil factory and an asbestos mine. To compensate him for his assets, the Russian government paid him with an equal value of artifacts from the Tsar.

In my assessment, the doctor was apolitical. Everything he did was to fulfill some purpose of his own, but never because of his belief in any "*ism*" but capitalism. There is no question he was helpful to the United States in our government's continuing dialogue with Russia, but again, he only did this for his own varied interests, which were vast.

The doctor and others have written books and articles about him that outline the most amazing things he was involved in during his lifetime, and some question the motives for which he did them. He was a throwback to the earlier days when the oil industry began with men like John D. Rockefeller. Some of his activities would have seemed more normal if he had done business in Rockefeller's time.

His career was probably as diverse as anyone I have ever heard of or known. His access to people around the world was more extensive than anyone I have known. When operating in foreign countries, it is difficult to work your way up the government chain to where business decisions are made. But with Dr. Hammer, you had to work your way down the chain because he always started with a king, premier, emir, or crown prince.

It was always interesting to travel with him. A couple of us went with him a variety of times to Mexico. A bevy of limos would meet us and then take us to the palace with a police escort. After our meeting, Dr. Hammer would leave, and we would stay behind to clean up whatever had been spilled. When we would leave the next day, we were totally depressed as we struggled in traffic, trying to reach the airport in our car.

When we flew with him to Arab countries, it was not unusual to be met by ten brand-new Mercedes. You had to remember that this was not the real world, and he only had to leave the country for us to find that out quickly.

Dr. Hammer loved to eat, and it never showed up much in his weight. He had a way of making up for his love for food by exercising and dieting. I was with him on a three-day trip to Abu Dhabi, Qatar, Bahrain, and Kuwait. We got to Bahrain in time for lunch, and a large group of people was assembled. Most of the food had been flown in from somewhere else since almost nothing is grown in that country. I thought the abundance of appetizers was the meal, but then we sat down for a full course lunch!

The doctor ate everything. At the end of the meal, they served what appeared to be a local version of bread pudding. I ate one bite and quit. It was delicious, but I was stuffed. I watched in amazement as the doctor ate his entire serving, and when we left the gathering to go to the plane, his aide was carrying a box that held four additional servings of the dessert. Before our trip ended, he had eaten them all!

When you went to a foreign country with the doctor, something had to take place that would result in a press announcement that involved him. His name had to appear in every positive news item that circulated within the company or in public. If the news was not so good, it was time for someone else to be introduced! That trait was not unique to him in the corporate world, however.

If you traveled to Washington, DC, with the doctor, two things were certain: you were going to stay at the Madison Hotel, and you were going to eat Maryland crab cakes with him, regardless if you were allergic to shellfish. You would normally eat those in his suite, where they had installed two heating systems especially for him. This way the temperature would be eighty-five degrees no matter what season of the year. At least it kept the food warm and the doctor happy.

It was standard that the doctor did not understand anything you did apart from working for him, and you could not escape him either. If you thought he did not know where you were, he would find you. For years, I played in the Canadian Oilmen's Golf Tournament. It was a great opportunity to create some special friendships in the industry while doing something I enjoyed, and it was by far the best organized event I ever attended. Of course, the doctor could not understand why I would take off for a week and play golf. The first time I played in the tournament after Oxy purchased Cities, he called me out of the opening dinner. He had no objective in mind. He just wanted me to know he knew where I was.

Another time, I was with an industry group, fishing in East Texas. I was in a very small motel that did not have individual phones in the rooms. The afternoon I arrived, I got a message that the doctor wanted me to call him in Birmingham, Alabama, at 11:30 p.m. that evening. The only phone that allowed me to do that was a pay phone on the wall of the small store attached to the motel.

At the appointed time, surrounded by trailers and RVs, I called the doctor in Birmingham. He could not understand where I was or what I was doing there. He wanted me to pick up my gas contract expert and be in Louis Nizer's office in New York City the next morning for a meeting. It was too late in the evening to argue with him, so I had the plane pick up the gas contract expert, who just happened to be at a meeting in San Antonio, at 2:30 a.m. and me in Shreveport at

3:30 a.m. We made the meeting in New York City at 9:00 a.m., and nothing that took place was worth the trip. Nevertheless, the doctor was pleased.

I wondered if he ever slept. One time, after a long board meeting that ended at 7:00 p.m., he was going to have dinner with Louis Nizer. As we exited the boardroom, the doctor told Louis that he had to go to his office and make a call and that it would take about twenty minutes. After he left, Louis said the doctor had been doing this to him for years. He said, "If you go to his office, you will find that he is asleep on his sofa. After twenty minutes, he will be refreshed, and I still will be tired." I honestly believe that is how he slept, in twenty-minute stretches during the day and night.

Armand Hammer was different from anyone I have ever known. I am not sure he even recognized the word *can't*. He always seemed to think that if you couldn't do something, then you weren't doing it right or you weren't smart enough. In most cases, he was probably right. He lived a big life, accomplished many things, and was successful by most people's standards. But in the end, all of his wealth and fame was left behind. He just pointed to Jesus and departed this world, a lesson to all of us.

CHANGING DIRECTION

The Doctor's death in December of 1990 brought about many changes at Oxy, which our new CEO, Ray Irani, began to implement within three weeks. As the new year of 1991 arrived, we took measures to reduce our debts. We reduced the stock dividend from $2.50 to $1.00. Then we set about selling $3 billion of assets. If there was one thing Oxy could do quicker than anyone, it was to either purchase or sell assets.

We turned to the North Sea. After the Piper Platform explosion, we had put together a plan to rebuild it. The project was not cheap. My group in Bakersfield estimated it would cost a little less than a billion dollars. I knew they knew this was grossly understated, but that is the way they worked. After the doctor's death, the platform was about 50 percent finished. We defined its market value and made our North Sea operation the number one sale target.

When faced with the problem of paying down debt, some companies try to sell what they don't want without accepting the fact that the market doesn't want that asset either. At Oxy, we always focused on what *would* sell. Dale Laurance had worked closely with a French company on other deals over the years, and we knew they wanted to be an oil and gas operator in the North Sea. Therefore, they became our primary prospect. As we did our own evaluation of the present net worth of

Piper, we could never get to anything over $1 billion, but Dale completed the sale to Elf Acquitane two months later at a price of around $1.5 billion.

This sale begs the question: when you know something is worth a given amount and someone is willing to pay 50 percent more than your assessment of its value, is there an implied obligation to ask them why they would do this? As I thought this over, they had access to a data room with all the information we used in our own evaluation, and they used this information in their calculations. As in many cases, they probably saw opportunities we did not see, and may have used a different price file or estimate of the future price of oil. They also paid a premium on becoming an operator in the North Sea for the first time. To conclude that they did not know what they were doing would be presumptive on our part, so there were no ethical questions that went unanswered. There was no misrepresentation of facts, just a difference of opinion on what an asset was worth.

※ ※ ※

In early 1991, as we were undergoing so many changes at Oxy, I took my yearly physical at Cooper's Clinic in Dallas and got a clean bill of health. About a month later, I applied for additional life insurance, and as usual, they requested a physical. They would not accept my latest physical from Cooper's Clinic. I called my physician in Tulsa, Fred McNeer, and told him I would send him a copy of my physical from Cooper's if he would use it to fill out the insurance forms. He said he would only do that after his own examination. With great reluctance, I consented.

Shortly after my exam, he called and told me everything was fine except my PSA, which was above normal. I replied that I had no idea what a PSA was. He explained that the PSA level might indicate whether there is a problem in the prostate, and he recommended I see an urologist. One of our close friends was an urologist, so I went to see Dr. Harold Calhoon. He did an ultrasound and then five biopsies, which all turned out to be negative. My PSA at that time was 6.3, which meant there might be something troublesome going on. He said he wanted to see me in six months.

In September 1991, I went in for my second prostate check. My PSA was down to 3.8, which was in the normal range. I have since found out that there is no normal range. After five more biopsies, Dr. Calhoon said he would call me by 4:30 p.m. the next day with the result. When he failed to call, I was certain as to why and called him on my way home. He hesitatingly asked me to come by his office. I knew then that cancer was present. When he confirmed my thoughts, we discussed what was next. I went through a bone scan and a CAT scan, which were both negative, and ultimately decided that surgery was my best option. The next question was where to have it done.

Dr. Calhoon did not operate at Saint Francis Hospital where I had been on the board for eight years. If I decided to have the surgery in Tulsa, I wanted to have it there. My other objective was to find a surgeon who did this operation so many times during the course of a year, and had done it for enough years that he would have seen everything and know how to deal with any problem that occurred. In 1991, there was no one in Tulsa that fit that description. Actually, at that time, there were few in the country with that degree of experience.

A doctor who worked for Occidental Chemical had spent some years at the Mayo Clinic and was very familiar with all phases of their system. He arranged for me to go to Mayo's for a 9:00 a.m. appointment with a surgeon in Rochester, Minnesota. I would then fly to Baltimore for a 3:30 p.m. appointment the same day with Patrick Walsh. He was the current guru of prostate surgery and was resident at Johns Hopkins. The protocol he had developed to avoid nerve damage was being used all over the world. After meeting the two doctors, I would decide where the surgery would take place. Suffice it to say, I had never met either of them.

These doctors were two of the best in their field. I prayed and asked God to show me which direction to take. I wanted a clear sign from him so that I would know it was his decision, not mine. What happened was remarkable. I was sitting in the exam room at Mayo's, waiting to see the doctor whom I had never met. He walked into the room, and we looked at each other with astonishment. He and I were wearing the same very unique Hermes tie. It turned out he had bought his two days before in Antwerp, Belgium. I had mine for two or three years and had just pulled it out of my closet at random that morning. I had never been aware of another person wearing the same tie I was wearing, and instantly, I knew God had answered prayer once again. How many times have I heard people say, "What a coincidence," when I know it's a God thing!

One of the questions I asked both doctors was "Can I assume that if I had this operation from any other doctor who does the operation the same number of times you do, that the results would be the same?" The Mayo doctor's answer was yes. He also named about eight doctors around the country who would fall into that category, including the doctor in Baltimore.

That afternoon, I posed the same question to the doctor in Baltimore. His response was that he had developed the technique, had done the surgery more often, and no one could do it as well. At first, I thought his remark was a little bit arrogant. When I thought about it more, it appeared to be reasonable considering he had invented the procedure that was used throughout the world. Both men were great surgeons, but God had indicated his choice. No one could have trumped the Mayo doctor's tie!

The next thing to decide was when the operation would take place. It was September, and at the end of October was the Tulsa Run, a fifteen-kilometer race I had run every year since it had begun thirteen years earlier. I was not going to miss this year for some dinky little reason like cancer. I also had an Oxy board meeting in early December. So we scheduled the surgery for November 12 at Mayo's.

The doctor wanted me to give two pints of blood to be transported to Mayo's in case there was excessive bleeding, which was a nice thought! This meant I had to give two pints of blood two weeks before the Tulsa Run. I asked the doctor if the run would be a problem for me. He said he would not run it under these conditions. I reminded him that what he would do was not my question. He said, "You can do it if you drink lots of liquids after the last vampire episode." I did so and ran—using the term loosely—the race. My consecutive string of this run was intact, but I set no personal record.

As Clydella and I were leaving for Rochester the day before the operation, I was called to the phone. To my surprise, it was Chuck Colson, who wanted to pray for me. Was I blessed or what? There were so many people praying for me that I did not have to pray for myself. It is a wonderful blessing knowing that because of God's love for us, we do not have to worry about cancer or other diseases. This life is just a dot on a line that is endless, and he watches out for us while we are here.

Everything went well with the surgery. The first thing I was aware of when I woke up was that there were thirty-five staples running from my navel to who knows where. My first thought was not whether the pathology report was positive or negative, but *how do they get those staples out?* I could only think of the staple-puller in my desk, and that thought was not pleasant.

While at Mayo's, I received thirty-five sprays of flowers during my short stay. I know that is hard to believe, but it is true. Dale Laurance sent one every day for four days. I finally called and cried uncle. The question in my mind was what to do with them when we left for Tulsa. Having volunteered in hospitals for years, Clydella knew exactly what to do. She roamed the halls learning about the situations of the other patients and delivered flowers to their rooms. She advised me every day that I was the luckiest one on the floor, which I had no reason to doubt.

We became friends with the staff, which was not hard to do because of the quality of the people there. While I love Saint Francis in Tulsa, Mayo's is almost in a category of its own. Medical personnel go to Rochester just to work there. The Mayo Clinic was originally built to serve the farming population of the surrounding area, and they still run the hospital with that personal care in mind.

With this surgery, and when I had had a disc removed from my lower back in 1969, I did not know anyone who had the same surgery and could advise me. Nevertheless, I was never worried about what went on during the surgeries. I wanted to know what happened *afterward*, and in most cases, the doctor had never done to himself what he had done to others, including me.

Probably the worst thing about recovering from prostate surgery at that time was that for three weeks, I had a catheter. This is like being tied up because you are. When the time came to remove the catheter, I decided to have my friend, Dr. Calhoon, do it. He is the same guy who walked into the examining room on my first visit with a machete. When I came in to have him extricate me from the catheter, I asked, "Is this going to be painful?"

He answered, "Not at all!"

I asked, "Have you ever had a catheter?"

He gasped, "I would never let anyone do this to me!"

Thankfully, he removed it without any discomfort at all.

My next concern was attending the Oxy board meeting, which would occur two weeks after I returned to Tulsa from Mayo's. Some adjustments were in order. In most cases, after the removal of the catheter, you are like a newborn baby. Fortunately, the period of time in which you have no control is normally short. Unfortunately, it extended into the time of the board meeting. Although many of the members on the board were over eighty, I liked to think I was the only one in the meeting wearing a diaper. I did not think it appropriate, however, to ask for a show of hands to make me feel more comfortable!

These experiences taught me to share information with others who were going to go through the same surgery I had gone through. Over the years, I helped about fifty people, letting them know what they could expect after the surgery, about which most doctors had no idea. I can't do this anymore, however. Now there are lasers, laparoscopes, robots, and the advent of new techniques, so my information has become outdated.

* * *

The events of 1991 had been stressful with the surgery and all the changes being made at Oxy after the doctor's death. During the year, I also managed to become involved with one of Clydella's charitable works. For seven consecutive years, she had been a vice chair of each of the seven United Way units in Tulsa, working to meet the goal of the yearly campaigns. After heading up all the individual units, she decided to move on and do something else because she knew they would never give a woman the job of campaign chairperson.

In the fall of 1991, I got a call from one of the board members of the Tulsa United Way. He told me the board wanted me to be the chairman of the campaign for 1992. My first response was "You called the wrong Hentschel! Clydella is the one who has worked in the campaigns for the last eight years. All I did was write checks." The person on the phone said the board wanted me to head the campaign. I said, "Call me back in ten minutes."

I told Clydella about the phone call and said I would not do it. Even through her disappointment, she said I must go ahead. When he called back, I said, "The only way I will agree is if you make Clydella and me co-chairs of the campaign."

There was silence on the other end, followed by, "I will call you back." When he called back, he said, "We think that will work." We became the only couple in the history of the Tulsa United Way to operate as a chair team, and Clydella was the only woman involved at that level until recently. Needless to say, after all the years she had given to their organization, she deserved the promotion!

The decision to be co-chairs worked out very well, primarily because of Clydella's experience and ability. Since I was traveling a great deal, she led meetings and oversaw everything in a very efficient and productive manner while I was away. The campaign was successful and never lost a step when I was gone.

It was fun to see Clydella in her element. For example, I believe 1992 was the first year of the Day of Caring, where companies came together for a day to provide services to the agencies in the United Way. When we explained the event to the board, we informed them that we needed to raise $20,000 to fund the expenses of that caring day. Almost without skipping a beat, Clydella took the floor and looked right at Hans Helmerich, a close friend and the CEO of Helmerich and Payne. She said, "Hans, why don't you give $1,500?" Hans said he would do so if Dave would do the same. Before you knew what was happening, she had raised almost all of the money from the board!

This was a great experience for both of us, and it also added some interesting challenges to our lives. One day, we awoke to the clock radio expounding on the story that the president and CEO of the United Way of America had just been indicted for embezzling money from the United Way of America to fund his bad habits. You can imagine what impact that had on the national campaign and Tulsa was no exception. Nevertheless, we only missed our goal of $16 million by about 6 percent.

As 1992 came to a close, I was aware that the collective strain of reducing our workforce, my recent surgery, and all the changes at Oxy had drained me of energy. It was affecting my ability to work as efficiently as I had in the past. It probably was not apparent to anyone else, but I could feel myself losing ground.

As I assessed my future, I knew if I was going to get control of the international business, I needed to move to Bakersfield, California, where few would welcome me. Moreover, neither Clydella nor I wanted to move.

Then, hanging over my head was the question about whether I would have any further bouts with the big C. For all these reasons, I decided to retire in 1993. I hated to leave Dale, Ray, and Oxy, but I was convinced I was not doing the job for which I was being paid. After I retired, it was no surprise to me that the person who took my place relocated the worldwide oil and gas operation from Tulsa to Bakersfield.

The rest of 1993, I tried to fish and play golf to occupy my time. Travel was never an objective of ours since we both had traveled to a large extent for the last fifteen years. Clydella and I automatically became co-chairs of the United Way board after our work in 1992. Fortunately, by then, people had forgotten the mishap with the president. Also, we were secure knowing that the governing deficiencies in the national organization had been corrected.

Even with my involvement in the United Way, it did not take long for me to lose the burnout and want something more to do than golf and fishing. I stayed close to Dale and thus informed about Oxy, but with very little thought that I would return to work or get involved in anything else that was very extensive. Then Hans Helmerich called.

Back in late 1992, I had received a call from Hans, who wanted me to chair an evangelistic crusade in Tulsa that was scheduled for late fall 1994. It would be led by a guy named Luis Palau. I had no idea who Palau was, and at that time, I was not looking for something else to do. I gave him some lame excuses to explain why I could not do it. When he called again in 1993, I had decided I might have made a mistake in retiring. He probably asked if I had any more lame excuses to keep me from doing the job, and I told him I would do it.

My only condition to Hans was that I needed to meet Luis Palau to confirm that he and I were on the same page. It would be more accurate to ask whether I was on Luis's page rather than the reverse! Meeting Luis and the other people around him would be one of those very special blessings from the Lord. I was asked after the crusade to go on Luis's board of directors, and I have been a part of his ministry ever since.

Preparation for the crusade was totally different than what I had anticipated. This was Tulsa, the heart of the Bible Belt. I believed it would be no problem getting church support for bringing an evangelical message to this wonderful city. I was wrong.

Churches in Tulsa have always been very independent of each other. They do wonderful work within the confines of their church, but have little desire to work collectively.

Sometimes, we forget we are the *body* of Christ, each member connected to the others by the blood of Jesus that binds us together. Jesus did not say we should split up into different groups, work separately, and believe the sum of what we did would be what he wanted. He prayed for us to be one and promised that when we worked together as one, what we could accomplish would be unlimited. It is for this reason I believe the world (and particularly America) is in its present state: the Church has been divided and thus unable to carry out Jesus's commands in a united effort.

The other thing that threw me during the preparation for the crusade was my inability to bring the African American community into the process. I started out with that as a main objective and tried very hard to see this happen. In the end, I took full responsibility for failing to do so, and it grieved me that so much of our past history still separates even believers in Jesus Christ. This experience made me even more eager to work to break down all barriers between churches and believers.

The crusade came and went, and I found myself disappointed with the results. Then one day, it became evident to me that the crusade had not been held for my benefit, something I wished I had realized sooner. God used it in so many ways I would never understand. How stupid I was to think otherwise!

During the next few years, the Palau board changed the format for evangelizing. The new festival format, which is still being used, has drawn crowds of over 300,000 over a two-day period in the United States and almost one million over the same period internationally. A festival generally reaches a larger and younger crowd by showcasing contemporary Christian music. Once there, they hear the special life-changing message of Jesus Christ as given by Luis Palau.

Clydella and I were amazed when we saw about 200,000 people at the festival on the beaches of Fort Lauderdale, Florida, one year during spring break.

They listened to the message of salvation sandwiched between some really great contemporary Christian groups. They are particularly loud, and someone asked Luis once whether he liked the music. He answered, "No, but I like the people that like the music."

Some of the people who not only like the music but perform it are nearly related to him. Amanda and Wendy Levy are daughters of Robert and Judy Levy, a very successful family in Jamaica. Wendy is married to Luis's son Andrew, and Amanda is married to Kevin Michael McKeehan. He is one of the most successful contemporary Christian musicians in the world, better known as TobyMac. His original group was DC Talk, which brought Christian rap to the forefront of the music business. Now Toby and his friends in contemporary Christian music are the magnets to draw young people to the festivals where Luis and Andrew tell them about God's love and redemption in Jesus. What a combination!

* * *

By the time Hans Helmerich had called me again to get me involved in the Luis Palau Crusade, I also had accepted a request to be a vice chairman for the 1994 PGA Tournament held at Southern Hills Country Club in Tulsa. There are two things that are known about a PGA Tournament in Tulsa in August: it will be hot and it will be well run. Unfortunately, the recent one held here in 2007 was run almost exclusively by the PGA, and in my opinion, it was not run as well or as efficiently.

There also is something very special that happens on the PGA Tour that is not known by the general public, and that is the Tour Bible study. Originally started by a group of players, including Jim Hiskey, Larry Mize, and Kermit Zarley, about thirty or more years before, they early on sought a person to be the study group's teacher, pastor, counselor, and avid supporter. They selected Larry Moody, and they did a much better job than we did at picking executives from the outside! I got acquainted with Larry Moody shortly after he started. He, his wife Ruthie, Clydella, and I have become close friends through our relationship with Jesus Christ. He has done an amazing work with the players who seek to know the Father better and live Christlike lives.

I have been privileged to see the influence Larry and Ruthie have had over the years. I also have gotten to know many of the players and have been part of some special outreaches associated with the tournaments in Tulsa. In 1994, at the PGA Tournament, one of my favorite memories took place when Paul Azinger spoke. In 1993, he had won the PGA tournament, but later in the year, he had been diagnosed with lymphoma and went through a very difficult series of chemotherapy treatments. As the media day in March of 1994 approached, Paul was progressing well but had lost all of his hair.

Clydella and I decided we would fly to Sarasota and pick up Paul and his wife Toni. We also picked up his agent and his wife, Robert and Dixie Fraley, who would also become good friends. Robert was a very special guy. He reflected all the godly qualities each of us desires in our life. The media day went well, and I got to take Paul in a cart around Southern Hills to see the course for the first time.

As a part of the week of a major tournament, there is always an evangelical outreach planned. The special prayer breakfast prior to the 1994 PGA Tournament featured Paul as the speaker and is still remembered by the 805 people who attended. I know how many were there because Mike Carter and I had planned the event. It was held in the Southern Hills Marriott's largest ballroom, which was filled to capacity.

Paul was especially good that morning and was supported by a large cast of Tour players. He gave his amazing and emotional testimony as to what God had brought him through during the previous months. He was never a real contender in the tournament because he was still struggling to regain his strength, but his talk that morning was unforgettable.

The next night at the Tour Bible study, Larry was finishing up the lesson for the evening. At about 9:45 p.m., the door opened and in walked Byron Nelson. He heard that the study was still in progress. For the next forty-five minutes, Byron talked about his experiences with Jesus Christ and his deep faith. I don't think anyone moved or said a word during that time. It was one of those mile-marker moments. No one in the meeting that night would trade that experience for almost anything that happened that week.

Five years later, in October of 1999, I was in a meeting and someone came in to announce that Payne Stewart's plane, which was headed for the Tour

Championship, had lost contact with the ground and eventually crashed somewhere in North Dakota. No one survived. I knew before it was confirmed that Robert Fraley was on board because he was Payne's agent as well as Paul's. What a loss! Fortunately, some years before he died, Payne had accepted Jesus as his personal Lord and Savior. What is not known is that if Paul had won a few dollars more that year, he would have been on the same plane.

Needless to say, the 1994 PGA ran very smoothly, and I cannot speak too highly of all who contributed. Between this great event in the summer and the Louis Palau Crusade in the fall, I kept busy. The only question on my mind as 1994 came to a close was "What next?"

THE CANADIAN ADVENTURE

By the time 1994 was over, I was ready to do battle again. All I needed was a good fight. As they say, you had better watch what you wish for because you might get just that. My fight manager, Dale Laurance, was about to schedule a new bout, but to understand how this happened, we need to go back to 1983, when Oxy bought Cities Service.

* * *

Oxy and Cities each had a Canadian company, and everyone in the merger understood that the two companies had to become one company. Thus, Canada-Cities Service and Canadian Occidental were merged and called Canadian Occidental (Can-Oxy). I was very familiar with Cities's operations in Canada because for two years I had been responsible for it, along with our South American operations. For some time after the two Canadian companies merged, I wondered why the new company, Can-Oxy, was allowed to exist. There was hardly anything going on except the depletion of assets, and there were no growth prospects. It seemed reasonable to question how the company was being run and who was at the helm. The ship appeared to have no destination or, even worse, did not know where it was going. This problem ultimately would be improved through a plan designed by the head of Oxy's tax department.

After Oxy had purchased Cities Service Company, for legal reasons, it had maintained its corporate identity; it just held no assets. The head of Oxy's tax department came up with the idea that Oxy could put some of its assets into the corporate structure that was Cities, transferring five or six platforms in the Gulf of Mexico that were still prime properties with lots of remaining reserves. In this new company, we would establish a balance sheet that created the platforms as assets alongside the negative value of some $2 billion that comprised a lot of the premium Oxy had paid for Cities, which at the time was $23 per share more than the value of the stock. Then we would sell the new Cities company. The sale price, based on market value, would be much less than the balance sheet assets. This would represent a capital loss, which could be carried forward. Thus, the loss would allow Oxy to sell assets in the future tax-free as the capital gain would be offset by the capital loss. All of this was within the limits of the tax regulations currently in place.

The Doctor loved the idea, but he wanted to sell the assets of the new Cities's company to Can-Oxy, thus keeping everything in the Oxy family. Our tax expert was adamant, even in the doctor's presence, that this action would not pass muster. The company would have to be sold at arms length in a full-scale market auction. Fortunately, the doctor agreed. A data room was set up, and a schedule was put in place to do what needed to be done to consummate a sale.

After we ran the auction, there were three serious bidders. The highest bidder was Conoco, but there was one large hitch to their bid. They wanted nothing to do with the implied liabilities tied to Cities Service Company. The company was seventy-five years old, and no one knew whether there were problems from the past that might surface in the future. They never did, but for that reason, Conoco only wanted the assets. They would not accept that selling the assets as Cities, with whatever the implied liabilities were, was the only condition under which the transaction could be made within the current tax rules. They maintained this position over the next couple of months, but we did not respond to their bid.

Sometime while we attempted to change their minds, it suddenly dawned on everyone that we had run a full-market open auction, which established the market value of the company, and now we could sell it at that price to anyone, including Can-Oxy. That is exactly what we did. Ralph Bailey, Conoco's CEO at the time, will swear to this day that we had planned it this way. I never could convince him that it was his stubbornness that allowed us to realize we could do what Dr. Hammer wanted to do in the first place.

This deal was the first real growth for Can-Oxy since the merger of the companies. It also became a stepping-stone to growing the US segment of the Canadian company. Some of those platforms in the Gulf are still producing and have recovered much larger amounts of oil and gas than were estimated in the original valuation.

Next, Can-Oxy looked to expand in the international market.

* * *

In the mid-1980s, Oxy was able to acquire a block in what was then South Yemen, which at that time was controlled by the Russians. Shortly after this, our government ordered US companies out of South Yemen as a form of sanctions. Being an American corporation, Oxy could give up the block or find a way to be involved that did not violate US government sanctions. We chose to give the block to Can-Oxy, which was acceptable under the terms of the sanctions, since Oxy owned only 30 percent of the Canadian company.

While Can-Oxy was looking for ways to grow worldwide, they were not ready to handle the magnitude of the Yemen project. They could not proceed without more experienced people in their organization, people who could handle the scale of such a project if it were successful. The answer was for Oxy to transfer experienced people to Can-Oxy. This decision would change Can-Oxy forever, but also benefit Oxy.

The exploration of the Masila block in Yemen began with a large-scale seismic program. Seismic shooting over the block was not easy.[6] Since Yemen sits on the south end of the Arabian Peninsula, most people think of it as being flat and sandy. It is not known to most people that the capital of Yemen sits at 7,800 feet, so there is quite a drop-off from there to the Gulf of Aden at the south end of the peninsula. Seismic shooting is difficult when there is a quick, pronounced drop-off in elevation, and in most cases, it might not even be effective. Thus, it was not surprising that the results of the seismic shoot were not very enlightening.

Because the seismic survey did not indicate clearly where to drill, the management of Can-Oxy wanted to farm the block out to someone else. Fortunately, there were four of us on the board of Can-Oxy from Oxy. We told them to pick out their best shot and start drilling wells. It was not very long before the initial discovery was made. Then, as development was taking place, something happened that could have reversed our fortunes. Civil war broke out in Yemen. The end result was that the country was united, the Russians were gone, and we had supported the right side. I can't tell you how much a person like Larry Murphy, who was and remains good friends with the president of the country, is responsible for the special relationship that has lasted for over twenty years.

We continued to develop the Masila block in Yemen and were constantly surprised by what we found. It eventually was revealed to be a series of individual producing formations, a handful of fields at different depths that overlapped one another. The original and central production facility was designed and constructed to produce 120,000 BPD, with a recoverable reserve figure estimated to be in the 200 million barrel range. We were a little conservative. The cumulative production from the fields as of this date is over 1 billion barrels, with a top-producing rate that reached 250,000 BPD of oil. It is a truism that in good fields, they tend to get better with time.

The only hitch in the process was that during the development of the Yemen field and before production started, we were faced with having to hire a new CEO for Can-Oxy. I was a part of the search committee, and we used a headhunter that submitted some 150 people from around the world for us to examine. This number was reduced in stages as we delved into the backgrounds of the people. We eventually got down to four and began to scrutinize them more closely. The committee, along with the chairman of Can-Oxy, Ray Irani, and Dale Laurance, interviewed each of the candidates. We spent enough time cumulatively to come to a reasonable conclusion, we thought. We picked someone who looked to be exactly what we wanted.

We found out something that we probably had not known before. There are people who can be what they think you want them to be for the length of the normal interview process. It was only after we made our choice that we found out that where he wanted to go and where we were going were two different things.

It was considerably less than a year before we knew there was a large difference between the philosophies of the new CEO of Can-Oxy and the majority owner of Can-Oxy, which was Oxy. The board and management of Oxy wanted to grow Can-Oxy while the new CEO of Can-Oxy wanted to find a way to get rid of the majority owner (Oxy) and sell Can-Oxy to his great benefit. We also knew that a management change at this level should only take place after ensuring that the difference between visions was irreconcilable. Management changes at the CEO level put a company in a standstill for some time as it takes a while for the new person to reveal their style of management and gain acceptance from the employees. It becomes even more difficult if you are in the middle of a project that requires the full attention of the whole organization. In this situation, the discord lasted longer than it should have, probably for the same reason Dr. Hammer took so long to make his 1984 management change.

The Masila block in Yemen began producing in 1992 and became much more than we expected. Everyone was happy. The financial street loved the success. The only dark spot in the picture was the management situation that had no possibility of getting better. It continued to be a sore that was not going to heal, and that was the situation when I retired in 1993.

* * *

In early 1995, after my two projects in Tulsa were finished, it became evident to me and to Dale Laurance that I was ready to do something, which supplied the answer to the situation in Canada. I was the only one from the old search committee left, and since Clydella was now introducing me in Tulsa as Dave "Get-a-job" Hentschel, I agreed to take on the responsibility of Can-Oxy with the approval of Ray, Dale, and the board of directors. As the president and CEO of Canadian Occidental Petroleum in Calgary, my main objective would be to find, preferably inside the organization but outside if necessary, the people qualified to become a line of succession for the future.

There were certain advantages to making this move. By 1995, I had been on the Can-Oxy board for eleven years and knew them well. I knew the majority owner (Oxy) even better. I knew how Oxy's management thought and wanted things to be done. I also knew most of the people who were currently in management positions fairly well. And I was currently unemployed! The only disadvantage was that I had to move to Canada ; I should say *we* had to move to Canada, Calgary, Alberta, to be exact. During the process of discussing the possibility with Dale, I had not told Clydella as there was no reason to bring up something that might not happen. She knew something was up, but it remained in the air. When we were sure it was going to happen, Clydella and I were in Palm Springs where I was attending a Can-Oxy board meeting. Dale and I pretty much cornered her at dinner one night and told her about the move.

For her to move out of Tulsa after she thought I had retired was not a step in Clydella's plans! She had so many friends in Tulsa, and at this point, they went back decades. Together, they had served the community and, most especially, the children of Tulsa through the Children's Medical Center and its successors for many years. While we would maintain our place in Tulsa, she would be making a bigger sacrifice than I would. Later, when the announcement regarding this move came out, Clydella looked it over and said, "This says Mr. Hentschel will reside in Calgary. It doesn't say anything about Mrs. Hentschel." Those were terms she could agree to.

Nevertheless, during the board meeting in October 1995, I first became executive vice chairman of Can-Oxy. Dale created this temporary position in order to put me over the current CEO of Can-Oxy until I had a chance to explain to him what was going on, mainly that he was being terminated and I was taking his place. This sounds harsh, but he truly brought this on himself after being given many chances to play the game as a team member. He was not happy when I explained to him that he was no longer in charge, but we ended our relationship on terms where we understood each other.

Clydella was still not excited to make a move north, especially in the winter, so I went up ahead, began work, and looked for a place for us to stay. One day, I happened to run into a friend from Mobil, who leased a two-story condo in downtown Calgary that was owned by a lady in London. He was transferring to Houston and would be vacating the condo very soon. I arranged to look at it, liked it, and was able to lease it at a reasonable price. It was on the twelfth and thirteenth floors of the building, and the master bedroom's west wall was all-glass, facing the mountains. Since we liked our high-rise in Tulsa and the new condo was five blocks from my office, this was a perfect solution to our housing needs. It also solved the problem of how to entice Clydella to come to Calgary in the winter.

I called Clydella and told her the condo was about 3,300 square feet and *needed to be furnished*. She was on the plane early the next morning and soon became close friends with a nice lady at Ethan Allen. They took two months deciding how badly they could hurt me. I learned my fate in February of 1996 when Clydella called me at the office and said, "Meet me at Ethan Allen at noon." When I pulled into the parking lot, she was standing in about two feet of snow, waiting for me. She told me in no uncertain terms that I was not to walk in and say, "What is the bottom line on this deal?" She said I was to listen and absorb what they had accomplished over the last two months.

Two hours later, and somewhat impressed with what they had done, I finally got the nod that I could ask what the bottom line was. Ethan Allen prides themselves in not making deals, but we did. It was six months later that the final item was delivered, a sofa that was made in their plant in Oklahoma! We kept saying we could drive down and get it much quicker, but the end result was very nice. We actually brought some of the furniture back to Tulsa and have it in our apartment today. However, most of it went to friends or children of friends as part of Clydella's "furniture ministry."

All of Clydella's volunteer work in Tulsa continued, and she flew back and forth to fulfill her responsibilities there. She enjoyed the people she met in Canada, but she would continue to be involved in the organizations she was part of in Tulsa. This arrangement was okay with me because it kept her busy and happy, and we both knew our time in Calgary would not last long.

* * *

I found it interesting to be back in the middle of a vibrant organization. It was fun to return, but I had to get used to the stress associated with being in charge of such a large complicated worldwide organization again. It is not easy to explain this to someone who has not been there. Some tend to think it is all perks and fun, but the majority of my career I was in the office at 6:00 a.m., stayed until 5:00 or 6:00 p.m., and left with a briefcase full of papers to contend with when I got home. Over the years, I traveled about 50 percent of the time, increasingly to overseas locations. I was blessed most of that time to be in a private plane, but that just means you get there quicker and get back faster so you can make the next trip.

There was no corporate plane at Can-Oxy, so all of my travel was commercial, and one of my responsibilities involved a lot of it. I became the company spokesman to the financial street and to our shareholders. A typical trip would be Calgary to Boston, then New York City, then Toronto, then Montreal, way over to Vancouver, and then back to Calgary. In each of those places, I would make a presentation of forty-five minutes to one person, a handful of people, or a roomful of people, and I would do that as much as five to seven times per day in some of the cities.

It is safe to say that after doing this five times a day, on the sixth time, I sometimes forgot what I had just said. I often wanted to say something completely off topic just to see if anyone was listening, or ask someone, "What did I just say?" not to see if they were listening, but to find out what I had just said! These meetings were time-consuming but important. It was also necessary that at least one time per year I did this internationally. It did not take me long to stop looking forward to the next trip.

Another challenge I faced was that the shareholders in Canada had recently employed the services of a couple of consultant groups to represent their collective interests. I learned very early that they did not like a non-Canadian running a Canadian company. They also did not like the fact that my professional history was tied to Oxy because Oxy was still the majority shareholder.

I met with them a couple of times to discuss their concerns and hear their complaints, but I made no concessions concerning the situation. American or not, I was there to do a job, and I had been with Oxy, the *majority shareholder*, for many years. They also had a growing concern about large corporations in general, and they wanted to know our plan to replace certain members of the board who were ready to retire. It was their desire to take part in the selection process. Since there was a good chance the people they would have in mind would be the same people we would look at, I asked them to furnish me with a list of people who were acceptable to them. My assessment was accurate, and we chose people who were on both of our lists.

As for the workforce, the first thing I did when I took over in Calgary was to call a meeting of the top two or three layers of management. I wanted them to know immediately what I was about. While most of them knew me from a distance, I wanted it to be more personal. I told them why I was there. It was not to further the career of Dave Hentschel. I was not there for personal gain, but to help them understand how capable they were. It was my job to create an environment where their talents could blossom. I also was not there for a long stay, but to set up a line of succession, and I was sure it could be done internally.

I have always believed in the team concept. It works well if you are open to giving credit to those who are really responsible for the success you achieve. I did not suffer long those who did not play the game with this in mind. It is not earthshaking that a group of people working well together will be more successful than if they work independently. It's the theory that 2+2 adds up to something more than 4.

It was also my responsibility to not only lead them, but also to give them whatever they needed to succeed and to provide an environment where they could reach their highest potential. I told those in management that my door was always open. If they had a problem, I was there to discuss it and help them find an answer.

I finished by letting them know that in my experience they were as talented as any organization I knew. It didn't take long before they understood what I said was true. I was not embellishing; I was stating the facts. Things could not have been better from an operations standpoint. We were in full production in Yemen and continued to find that many of the individual fields were larger than we originally had thought. We also continued to have good relations with the Yemen government, thanks to Larry Murphy. There was only one blip on the Masila screen.

As I indicated earlier, the original plan for the development of the Masila field was based on a maximum production of 120,000 BPD. The production facility for that amount was originally estimated to be in the neighborhood of $400 million. As we continued to develop the field, it was evident that production would actually be in excess of 200,000 BPD. Thus, the production facility would have to be larger as well, increasing the cost to around $800 million.

Our contract with the government was a cost recovery agreement in which 40 percent of the oil production was returned to Can-Oxy to repay the money invested. The rest of the oil was divided on a sliding scale basis with the major portion going to Yemen. While Yemen was happy with the increase in production, they were not happy with the increase in the cost of facilities, which would mean more money for us. They wanted to reduce the cost recovery account by the difference between the initial estimate and the final cost. You can see why this issue required some degree of diplomacy. They did not want to accept the fact that a facility to produce 250,000 BPD costs more to build than one that produces half that amount.

One of the extraordinary traits of Oxy, attributed to Dr. Hammer, is that they could get things built in a time frame that was faster than anyone in the business. If Oxy said first production would take place on a given date, you could be sure it would happen on that date. They were able to move so fast because they overlooked the added cost of doing things more quickly. There always was a target for first production, but there never was a target for total cost. "Whatever it takes" was the approach.

They justified speed and greater cost by the fact that the sooner they started producing, the sooner they would make a profit. This benefit would far outweigh the additional cost. In most cases, if you were in a market where the price of oil and gas was rising, this was true.

After the production facility at the Masila block in Yemen was completed, we evaluated the difference between the two construction numbers. One hundred million dollars of the additional cost was attributed to a rush to production. The number sought by the government was $150 million. In the end, Larry and I figured out a way to arrive at that number by prepaying some future costs that made both parties equally happy or unhappy as the case might be.

With all these challenges, I found the staff at Calgary to be exemplary. It didn't take long for me to know that choosing a line of succession would be no problem. Already, Can-Oxy had two people in place who would become that line. My job was to sell the majority shareholder, Oxy. By midyear, Ray and Dale were in agreement.

* * *

One of the things I was going to miss when we made the move to Canada was the Bible study in Tulsa I had been a part of since 1980. We met every Wednesday morning at Southern Hills Country Club. I have found it very helpful to share God's Word with other believers.

A group like that allows you to be able to reaffirm weekly the foundation on which you are building your life. I needed some way to become involved with a similar group in Calgary.

In the mid-1980s, I had met a guy from Calgary named Kevin Jenkins at an outreach conducted by a mutual friend in San Diego. That friendship had continued, and by the time we moved to Calgary, Kevin was the CEO of Canadian Airlines. When I contacted him, he told me there was a Bible study each Tuesday morning in downtown Calgary at one of the largest law firms. I was there the next Tuesday and continued until I left. Amazingly, when I left Calgary two years later, I became a member of a men's Bible study in Bakersfield the first week of my relocation. The three groups were very different, but the Bible we studied and our desire for a closer relationship with Jesus were identical.

Kevin is one of those special people whom God has allowed me to know, and we have become real brothers in Christ. While I was CEO of Can-Oxy, I asked Kevin to become a board member. He was knee-deep in problems and had very little interest in being a director. I finally was able to convince him, and he has been a very valuable director on that board ever since. Recently, he was selected from a worldwide search to become the president and CEO of World Vision International. He and his wife Helen are in a position to do great things for God's kingdom, and Clydella and I are grateful to know them.

In early 1996, I was invited to a meeting in Calgary to discuss bringing an evangelistic outreach to the city.

The group wanted to bring Tom Lehman, a long-term member of the PGA Golf Tour Bible study, to speak. We pursued a commitment from his agent, who just happened to be his brother, Jim. Our group wanted to have the meeting in June or July. I reminded them that these guys were playing golf during that time. Furthermore, most of the majors took place between April and August, and if Tom happened to win one of those, his time would be limited. We proceeded to schedule him the first week in November of 1996. By the time the event took place, Tom would be the reigning British Open champion, which made his appearance even more special.

I arranged for Tom to spend the night with Clydella and me at our high-rise condo. He showed up in Calgary in November wearing shorts! Fortunately, he brought some long pants. I was totally amazed that we had almost 700 people show up to hear him. Calgarians love golf and they loved Tom. God blessed the event in that almost one hundred people indicated they accepted Jesus as their Lord and Savior for the first time. For months afterward, people were still talking about it.

* * *

In the last quarter of 1996, I was asked into a meeting to evaluate an opportunity that was going to become available in the very near future. The province adjacent to Alberta on the east is Saskatchewan. Early in its history, the province had created its own oil company. Some years later, as a means of raising money, they took that company public. It became Wascana, and the province retained a 10 percent interest. They also prohibited the other 90 percent ownership from selling their interests without the approval of the province or unless the government decided to sell their remaining interest.

At the time of our meeting, the Saskatchewan government had decided to sell their interest in Wascana in January of 1997, which meant the company would be up for sale. We wanted to acquire the company and its assets as they fit very well with our own properties in the area. Our group had done a great job of placing us in a good position to make the acquisition, but they also determined there would most likely be an attempt at a hostile takeover from someone else. We had no intention of being hostile because that kind of move is hardly ever successful. To be prepared for that happening, we proposed to discreetly start buying stock in Wascana. We could buy up to 5 percent of the outstanding stock without having to disclose our interest. Then, when the hostile offer came down, we could respond quickly with a "white knight" offer and proceed to see what happened. In the event we were unsuccessful in the acquisition, we could at least make some money based on the stock purchases. In November, the board approved the plan, and we began to buy Wascana stock.

By the time Talisman made the hostile offer for the company in early 1997, we had accumulated about 4 percent of Wascana stock. Talisman tendered for 100 percent of the company at $18.75 per share.

They proceeded to tell the financial market about the extremely detailed and intelligent basis on which they based that price and that no one in their right mind would top that offer. What they did not know is that the Can-Oxy board had already given me authority to go to $23 per share.

My first action after the hostile tender was to call the chairman of Wascana. I wanted him to know that we stood ready to make a counteroffer that would be better for all concerned. I think he greatly appreciated my call. Two weeks later, we placed an offer of $20 per share on the table. Talisman immediately took us to task in the press for having done such a dumb thing. After declaring no sane person would bid more than they did, they found themselves unable to eat their words and make a counteroffer. For the next few months, I continually received calls from the CEO of Talisman, asking us to trade the stock position they had lined up in their hostile offer for some of the assets that would benefit them. I avoided all of his calls and to this day have never talked to him.

Talisman was not the only player in the game we had to contend with. One Friday morning a few weeks later, the chairman of Wascana called and indicated there were other offers, and they needed our final price by Monday morning. With Vic Zaleschuk, who took my place as CEO after I left and was our CFO at the time, I contemplated what our final offer should be. When I told Ray Irani that we were going to bid $20.50 per share, he asked why I didn't go for the $23. I told him I did not think we would have to.

We called and changed our bid early Monday morning to $20.50 per share. For the rest of the day, Vic and I must have walked twenty miles around the inside perimeter of our floor, wondering why we didn't go to the higher bid. At 5:00 p.m., I got a call that Wascana wanted to meet with us and finalize the deal. Congratulations to a fine effort on the part of an organization that showed their very able skills! To be truthful, however, only after prices started to rise a few years later did we start to realize the value of the purchase.

* * *

In the latter part of 1997, Dale called about another problem that was surfacing at Oxy. The guy who had taken my place as CEO over all domestic and international oil and gas operations, which he had headquartered in Bakersfield, was not working out. This created a situation that required someone from outside the company to deal with the organizational problems. Dale had started a worldwide search for a candidate, and he asked for my suggestions. That search would take the better part of six months, and the candidate picture was not all that bright. When the search was narrowed down to one candidate, Dale asked me to have dinner with the candidate and his wife, which I did.

Again, we were convinced we had found the best person for the job, but in the back of Ray and Dale's minds loomed our failed assessment of hiring from the outside at Can-Oxy. Dale came up with a quick solution. Why didn't I, after finishing the job in Calgary in a couple of months, move to Bakersfield and oversee the new guy for a couple of years until it was determined he was a good choice? My first thought was that Clydella would love the idea. We enjoyed our time in Canada, but we did not look forward to another winter. Unfortunately, the two winters we were in Canada were the worst in many years. They would always say, "But it's a dry cold," as if that made a difference when both the Fahrenheit and centigrade crossed paths at forty below zero.

The last few months in Calgary were spent cleaning up everything associated with the Wascana purchase. By the time I left for Bakersfield, I had much to be thankful for. It had been fun and very educational to both watch and be a part of the transition Can-Oxy made from my first introduction to them after Oxy purchased Cities Service in 1982 to being a significant player in the domestic and international arena by 1997.

My service to Can-Oxy did not stop in 1997, however. I went back to being strictly a board member and continued until I was aged out at seventy-five after twenty-four years. This is certainly one of the dumb rules that corporations have imposed on themselves for a variety of reasons. One reason is that it is traditional. That is the way everyone did it in the old times, except Dr. Hammer, of course. I learned from my time on the Oxy board that there is great benefit to be gained from the wisdom and experience of older people. It is interesting to try and explain how the age rule on a Board does not really allow for the recognition that at a given age some directors are very capable of continuing to be very productive, and others are not. Regardless, the rule rules. After serving on the Board of Occidental and seeing people at the age of 85 continue to do well was a great lesson to me. Capable and committed Board members are not that easy to find. For whatever reason, Boards find it difficult to discriminate between a performing director and one that is not. This is ironic since most of them have spent their careers having to do just that in their own organizations on a daily basis. Maybe it is just sour grapes on my part.

And so I took my old job back in order to oversee the replacement, and we moved to Bakersfield, the move I avoided four years earlier by retiring. There was one special occasion that had nothing to do with work but for which I returned to Calgary. Late in 1996, I had been asked to speak at the Mayor's Prayer Breakfast in Calgary the following year in November 1997. Because the Canadian shareholders were not happy to have an American-named CEO of Can-Oxy, and there is such pride in the Canadian people that way, I was flattered and somewhat amazed by the request. I also knew it would be another opportunity for me to speak about my relationship with Jesus.

After I was relocated to Bakersfield in June of 1997, I called the person in charge of the prayer breakfast in Calgary to see if they wanted to change their minds since I was no longer there. They said they had not changed their minds and were looking forward to hearing me speak. Again, I was amazed. The breakfast saw some 400 people from the business and political world come together to listen to three speakers. This was yet another platform God provided for me to tell about Jesus. The following is an excerpt from my closing remarks at the breakfast:

> And most special to me is the fact that some 2000 years ago Jesus, with full knowledge of me and you and everyone who would come after Him, and the human failings that we all represent, laid down His life so that we can have eternal life. What a blessing!
>
> Seven years ago, I had the opportunity to walk where Jesus walked, to pray where Jesus prayed, to cry where Jesus died, and to celebrate where Jesus arose. Israel is a very special place for both Jews and Christians. What an experience! It confirmed to me that my life has been properly committed and properly focused on what is important. It confirmed to me that the search for money, power, and prestige does not create the kind of happiness and satisfaction for which we long. In my case, a close relationship through the person of Jesus Christ has made all the difference in who I am and the reason behind it.
>
> He can have the same impact on you. I would encourage each of you to open each compartment of your life to God. He will make the difference. It is not a difficult process to start a relationship with God. First of all, God loves each of you in a very special way. In John 3:16, we read, "For God so loved the world that he gave His only begotten Son, that whosoever believeth in Him should not perish, but have

everlasting life." And because of that love, God has made it very simple to come to know Him.

In Romans we read, "If you confess with your mouth the Lord Jesus, and believe in your heart that God raised Him from the dead, thou shall be saved."

As always, I was gratified at the response to this message. People were truly blessed by understanding the special relationship with Jesus that is available to anyone who desires it. The two newspapers reported the event and focused on my commitment to my Lord. I knew this had nothing to do with me. He provided the opportunity and then gave me the words to say to glorify his name.

AT LAST...BAKERSFIELD

In 1997, I returned to my previous position as chairman and CEO of Occidental Oil and Gas Corporation and began the next phase of my MBA degree in Bakersfield. The management of the worldwide oil and gas operations in Bakersfield went through some upheaval when the guy who had taken my place four years before and moved the worldwide headquarters from Tulsa to Bakersfield was gone. Not only would they have to deal with me being their boss again in Bakersfield, but the new COO I would groom for CEO was being brought in from another company and country. There were some who were not pleased.

My position was different than any I had had before. I was to oversee and mentor the new guy coming in, and he was never happy with that situation, but Ray and Dale did not care. They were more concerned with having someone they trusted confirm he was a good fit for the position. Initially, I could see the new man was suffering from culture shock. Coming from London, Bakersfield was not anything he had anticipated. The formality and pomp of his English experience collided with California informality. I think his first clue came when we went to a fund-raiser to raise money for Christmas toys. He went to the bar and asked what wine they were serving, expecting to hear the vineyard and the age of the wine. The answer he got was "Red, white, and pink."

In the meantime, the first thing Clydella and I had to do was find a place to stay. We had lived the last four years in high-rises and loved it, but a high-rise in Bakersfield was a two-story house. So we had to change our plans. We looked for a couple of weeks without success. Then we had to stop our search momentarily while we went to New York City for a dinner we had committed to attend. On Wednesday, Clydella went back to Tulsa to get ready. I was to pick her up in the company plane in Tulsa on Friday.

On Thursday morning, our realtor in Bakersfield called and said there was a house coming on the market on Monday that would be sold before noon that day. She said Clydella had to come back. I told her that was not going to happen and explained why, but I went to see the house. She was right. It was beautiful: one-story, 4,800 square feet, with a 1,500-square-foot covered patio looking out on a typical English garden. I said, "This is what Clydella wants."

She said, "Leave it to me," and that afternoon she gave me a forty-five–minute video of the house. I picked Clydella up in Tulsa on Friday as planned, and as soon as we were in the air, I put the video in the VCR. We watched it once and bought the house over Pittsburg! It was by far the best house we ever owned. If we ever decided to build a house, it would be the Bakersfield house.

While I met the challenges of dealing with our new COO and the somewhat disgruntled Bakersfield staff, we found the people of that city to be as friendly and kind as those in Tulsa. During her stay, Clydella was on the boards of the United Way, the Salvation Army, and the American Diabetes Association, so she had plenty to keep her busy. We truly enjoyed living there, and neither one of us missed the snow!

※ ※ ※

I was pleased to see that during my four-year absence from Oxy, the business had moved forward. Then another great opportunity opened to us, and Oxy became a contender for a very special property, the Naval Petroleum reserve at Elk Hills. The situation was much the same as Wascana. The US government had controlling interest in Elk Hills, along with various other oil properties in the country. This was because after World War I, they had realized the Navy required a safe and restricted supply of their own fossil fuel for the naval fleet, in this case, fuel oil. This was good thinking at the time, but in 1997, the Navy was totally fueled by nuclear power and had little need for fossil fuel.

I am not familiar with who did the original geology report, which led to the discovery of Elk Hills. Suffice it to say, it is probably the most anomalous field in California. In a region where the majority of oil is heavy and low gravity, Elk Hills was a 23,000-foot basin with a substantial gas cap and oil that was light, altogether much more desirable. Since the Department of Energy (DOE) was not in the business of developing hydrocarbons, the field had been operated since its development by Chevron, who owned approximately

25 percent of it. This relationship continued into the 1990s. Because the Navy's fleet was now nuclear powered, they announced that Elk Hills was for sale.

When I got there in 1997, a group had formed to evaluate our interest in bidding on Elk Hills. For years, the international headquarters of Oxy had been located in Bakersfield, and Oxy was a major player in the international arena. The committee was chaired and controlled by people who believed that the only place to find and produce oil was ten time zones away in either direction. To think that a potential underdeveloped field could exist thirty miles from Bakersfield took more imagination than was present on the committee. This was my challenge.

Dale and I were in Jasper, Alberta, for a Can-Oxy board meeting, when I explained the problem to him. He asked what I would do. My answer was that we should transfer the person who had run the committee to acquire Wascana to Bakersfield. He was most agreeable, but the people in Bakersfield would not be. Again, another outsider was coming in to lead the fold.

Mark Hauser had done a great job supervising the purchase study of Wascana in Canada. Now he was in Dallas, running the oil and gas operation for Can-Oxy's US operation. All we had to do was bring him to Oxy, and we would give ourselves the best chance of being competitive in the auction. Since much of the early success of Can-Oxy was based on bringing over more experienced people from Oxy, in some sense, it would be a great payback. The board of Can-Oxy had no problem with the idea. It was my job to talk Mark out of Dallas and into Bakersfield. Mark and I had become great friends, and I was very much aware of his potential. When I explained to him the basis for our request, he accepted. He joined us in the fall of 1997, and without his participation, our evaluation of Elk Hills would never have gotten off in the right direction.

The uniqueness of Elk Hills was not only the geology. The arrangement with Chevron was also unusual. Chevron, a minority owner, was the operator because the DOE had no ability to develop and manage an oil field. By the very nature of this arrangement, Chevron had to be frustrated by the difficulty in getting the DOE on board to do what needed to be done. For one thing, departments in the government do not understand dry holes. To be truthful, I have run into some management people in major oil companies that did not understand dry holes either. The government does understand buildings and cars, however, so it was no surprise to find all sorts of buildings and rolling stock when I first visited Elk Hills.

It was not hard to believe that Chevron and the DOE were at odds on many issues that had accumulated over the years. I think these differences, which could be translated to money, had an impact on Chevron's eventual bid for the property. In many respects, they should have been the winner of the auction.

Texaco also stood to gain tremendously from the acquisition. There was potential gas production that could significantly reduce their need to purchase gas in the open market, gas they used in their heavy oil production facilities. We worried about them as we proceeded forward.

The events that followed are extremely unique in matters such as these because everything happened so quickly. Mark's committee did a great job of evaluation, and as we approached the end of 1997, we were ready for the board presentation. The board was impressed with the opportunity and gave us approval to bid up to $4.3 billion. Now we had to determine what the actual bid should be based on anticipated competition. This is not entirely an analytical determination. At best, it is an educated *feel*. The objective is always to get the property and leave no money on the table and say a prayer for lots of luck. Many of us shared ideas about what the bid should be, but the final decision rested with Ray, Dale, and a few others. Our bid would be $3.65 billion.

An interesting thing happened six months after we had purchased Elk Hills. I had a visit from the Texaco person in Bakersfield. It was really a get-to-know-each-other visit. During the conversation, I asked why Texaco had not bought Elk Hills because they were the largest user of the additional gas we were producing. He told me he had headed the group that did the evaluation, and he had made the presentation to the Texaco board. His recommendation was to bid $4 billion. When he walked out of the meeting, he was handed a note from the CEO. It said, "Bid $3.5 billion." Since bids were never divulged in this type of sale, it was unusual to hear this bit of information.

You would suspect the government would be slow in responding to the auction bids, but the opposite was true. Immediately, the DOE selected Oxy as the winning bidder, and the purchase agreement was signed days later. There were some interesting things that transpired as we approached the closing of the deal, however. One of them was almost as funny as it was pitiful and even frightening.

Elk Hills had around 300 pieces of rolling stock on location. This included cars, pickups, and trucks of all sizes, showing that purchase of tangible goods was something the government understood, of course. I got a call from Dobie Langenkamp, a good friend from Tulsa, who was working in the DOE at the time. He explained that the rolling stock at Elk Hills had different ownership than just the DOE. The chassis of each vehicle was owned by the General Services Administration (GSA) while the operational equipment that had been permanently secured to each vehicle was owned by the DOE. Therefore, the operational equipment was now Oxy's, but the chassis of each vehicle was still GSA's. Furthermore, no GSA equipment could be sold until it was so many years old or had so many miles of operation on it, conditions that had not been met yet. Dobie had been trying to get approval for an exception to that regulation, exhausting all avenues to do this, but to no avail. I immediately flew to Washington, DC.

I had appointments to meet with a variety of senators and congressmen to see if they would help with a solution, knowing that if we couldn't get around this regulation, we would have to strip the operational equipment off the vehicles, return them to the GSA, and then bring 300 new vehicles on the property.

As I started my congressional rounds, explaining the situation, I became aware when I lost my audience. Their eyes would glaze over, and in the end, they would offer no solution. This went on all day. My last chance was Bill Thomas, a congressman from Bakersfield, who just happened to be the chair of the Ways and Means Committee. He came off the floor to see me at about 7:00 p.m. that evening. When I finished telling him my story, he began chewing me out. He said, "You should have called me much earlier. I would have had any number of bills to file the exception."

I said, "Does this mean you can't do it?"

He said, "No, it does not. I can still do it, but it will be more difficult." When he was able to get the exception passed, however, the bawling out I got was worth it. We proceeded with the Elk Hills purchase and closed the deal in Washington, DC, early in January 1998. We went through the traditional signing with the secretary of energy and received the signing pens as souvenirs. I have no idea where mine went. It must have not seemed important at the time. Then we began the transition as the new owner of Elk Hills.

There were environmental concerns that went way past my natural instincts. Elk Hills was a habitat for kit foxes and kangaroo rats. We had to ensure the concerned people that we would do nothing to disturb them. I wondered if the cities in the hundred-mile radius of Bakersfield had the same problem these environmental groups did. We saw kit foxes all the time on the golf course in Bakersfield, and they did not seem to have a problem adapting to the developed property. If those foxes could understand the concern about their welfare being registered by the special interest groups, they would probably laugh.

Going in, we understood some of the difficulties Chevron had in getting the DOE's approval to bring Elk Hills's natural gas to market, so we immediately laid a six-mile pipeline. This allowed us to increase the gas transported from under 100 MMCFPD (million cubic feet per day) to over 400 MMCFPD. At that time, the gas market was very strong, so our natural gas revenues increased substantially. This was the first of many changes that took place the first year.

* * *

In all this, I had been observing how our new COO was performing. He did not like being watched and evaluated, and he resented my relationship with Ray and Dale; nevertheless, we got along fairly well. As we neared the end of 1998, the price structure for oil and gas went into the tank. I think by that time, Dale and I had decided the positions at the top of the oil and gas unit were not necessary. Since Oxy was much less complicated, with only chemicals and oil and gas groups remaining, we decided the oil and gas unit should report directly to Dale. The chemical group was still reporting to Ray, so this new structure would simplify things. By the end of 1998, we moved to implement the new changes.

A significant change also happened to me personally that year. It does not follow that runners are smart about running! I was about to run the Tulsa Run for the twentieth consecutive time. For some fifteen years in Tulsa, I had trained with Chester Cadieux, a very special friend, as my running partner. The race would be his twentieth also. After we finished the race and I was back in Bakersfield, I called Chester and asked if we were going to do number 21? He replied that I could do what I wanted, but that was his last competitive run. I was relieved with his answer. After thirty years of running, my foot had broken down, and I had to have surgery to repair the damage. I recovered just fine, but after that, I had no interest in running again. I also knew my time in Bakersfield was coming to an end.

At the beginning of 1999, Dale offered me a new job in Los Angeles. I knew this was being done as a favor to me, but I also knew there really was no job. I would mostly be a sounding board for Dale. When I told Clydella about the Los Angeles possibilities, she simply told me to sit down and said, "I have followed you around the country for years. If I go to Los Angeles, I would have to be close to a mall because I will not drive in the city. You can go to Los Angeles, but I am going home." We had decided a long time ago that Tulsa was home.

I called Dale the next day and told him I very much appreciated his offer, that it would be fun to continue to be a part of all the things that would go on, but if he really had something in mind for me to do, I could do it just as easily in Tulsa. I think he was somewhat relieved with my decision, and it gave me a chance to go back to Tulsa and try retirement again.

I have always been grateful to Dr. Hammer, Ray, and Dale for giving me an opportunity to be a part of some very interesting years at Oxy. Ray and Dale are responsible for making Occidental Petroleum one of the most successful companies during my years in business and afterward. Those of us who saw what they inherited when Dr. Hammer died knew how much they had accomplished. Later, they took a chance on two very large oil and gas purchases, and their timing could not have been better.

It is always interesting to see the "Street" criticize asset purchases as being "overpriced." They never come back and say anything after they are proven wrong. The three purchases changed the makeup of the company from almost solely international to a very significant domestic producer as well. This benefited the company enormously when the price of oil continued a long rise.

Dale retired a few years back, and at this writing, Ray is still the CEO. I have no doubt Ray misses Dale. I would continue to "consult" for a while, and I was happy to continue my association with these wonderful men.

NEW ADVENTURES

When I retired and returned to Tulsa in 1999, I joined the board of Southern Hills Country Club. Southern Hills had hosted five major golf tournaments, including the 1994 PGA Tournament, for which I was vice chairman. Now we were looking forward to hosting the 2001 US Open. I served again as a vice chairman of this event, and we began preparations. Something very special happened during this experience, primarily due to Clydella.

One of the various responsibilities I had was contestant hospitality. Clydella was my selection to head this area! The most difficult part of this job prior to the actual tournament itself was to find a gift for the players that was not only unique, but that we could afford. We knew that if anything crystal was given, half of the gifts would be left in the lockers. Professional golfers are not short of crystal. At one tournament, large bottles of wine were given, most of which were left in the lockers. Almost anything you choose is something they have already been given many times.

When I related this very difficult problem to Clydella, I expected her to respond in a couple of days. She responded in seconds, "Why don't we get Roz Cook to do a bronze statue?"

I wanted to say that it isn't that easy. You can't come up with a good idea that quickly! Then it dawned on me that this might be the best idea anyone had in years, until the issue of money came to mind. Although a resident of Tulsa, Roz Cook is one of the best bronze sculptresses in the country. Her work was shown a great deal in Tulsa but also across the nation, and her work might be out of our available price range.

We called Roz and presented the problem to her. What we had in mind was a statue of a teenage golfer, standing by a golf bag and looking into the distance. Roz was not a golfer and was not very enthusiastic about the idea. She said she would call back. She talked to her husband Hal, who was a golfer. He said, "If you do this, Tiger Woods will have one of your sculptures." She warmed to the idea since she, and the rest of the world, knew who Tiger was.

Roz called to say that a thirteen-inch statue would have a foundry cost of $400. I said the most any club had spent on a gift was $150 per person. Since we would need somewhere in the vicinity of 175 statues, the cost was out of our reach. She said she would call back. After talking with Hal again, she called and asked, "Why not make a special issue of the statue to be sold within the membership of the club? If you could sell 125 of them for $1,200 each, $400 would go to the foundry, $200 to me, and the other $600 to fund the cost of the issue of the statues to the players and officials. Then it would be a breakeven proposition."

I presented the proposal to the board and got unanimous approval, and then again when I showed them the clay model. I named the statue "Someday," which is probably the thought every young golfer has as they look into the distance and dream of becoming a professional golfer and winning a major tournament.

Roz always used someone as the model for her statues. I knew Tom Lehman had a son about seven years old, so I called him. I asked if he and Melissa would allow Roz to use Tommy, aged to about fourteen years old, as the model. Almost immediately I received a bunch of pictures of Tommy.

The statue was a big hit with everyone, and we eventually sold about 300 of them to the membership at Southern Hills. Later, I attended the 2000 US Open at Pebble Beach. I showed Loren Roberts the first statue that had been produced to see what he thought of it. He said it would be the best gift from a tournament he had ever received. I still marvel at the fact that Clydella came up with the idea so quickly, and that Roz and Hal arrived at a workable deal to see the idea come to reality.

Young Tommy came into the pro shop in June of 2001 at the start of tournament week and was very enthused by the statue and his part in it. He should be more overwhelmed by the fact that his life-sized statue now sits at the entrance to the Club House at Southern Hills. Every time I see it, I see another God deal!

* * *

The 2001 US Open at Southern Hills was a great tournament. Retief Goosen won in an eighteen-hole playoff. Later, we decided to do some major renovations to the course, so I would be greatly involved in the plans. At the time, I was chairman of the greens committee, a position I held for five years. The most extensive work occurred as we prepared the golf course for the next tournament we would host, the 2007 PGA Tournament.

Our original thought was to replace the fairways and enlarge the practice putting green and the upper practice tee. The fairways, as a result of weather damage and subsequent replacement of the damaged grass over the years, were comprised of at least three different and distinct grasses. When you sat in the men's grill and looked down the ninth and eighteenth fairways, you could outline the border of each grass that was present because of the different color and texture of the grasses. The variance also showed up in the aerial shots taken during the 2001 US Open. It would take about eighty acres of sod to replace the fairways, and we hired Course Crafters, who would do the work in August of 2005.

Our course superintendent at that time was John Szelinski, and he noticed something very unusual during July of 2005. We were having a mild and wet summer, and under these conditions, the greens should have been doing well, but they were stressed. John cut fourteen-inch-deep cores from five different greens and what he found was even stranger. When placed side by side, you would think all the cores came from one green. They were almost identical. About eight to nine inches below the green surface, there was a 1- to 1-1/2-inch layer of clay that trapped water in the upper area and stunted the grass. The area below the clay was as hard as brick. No water had passed through for years, if ever.

We researched what had been done to cause this so that the mistake would not be repeated. We found that after the 1958 US Open, it was decided to rebuild the greens. The United States Golf Association (USGA) specification at that time was to put four inches of pea gravel above the underground drainage system, then twelve inches of growth mix. Moreover, the USGA worried that the nutrients used at that time might filter through the greens too quickly and thus be ineffective in helping growth and health. To prevent this, they recommended a one-inch layer of native soil, in this case clay, to be placed on the surface.

Over the years, with the sanding of the greens four or five times each year, the area above the clay had filled to eight to nine inches. This is what we found in every green we cored. If the condition was not corrected, we could lose many greens the year before the 2007 PGA Tournament and have almost no possibility of rectifying the situation beforehand. We needed to act quickly since Course Crafters would be there in less than two weeks. Based on the approval of the greens committee and the board, we changed the overall plan dramatically.

First, we decided to core out and replace every green. To do this effectively, we had to replace the drainage system underneath. We would reline all traps, put in new sand, redo the drainage and irrigation system throughout the course, and move the tee boxes on three or four holes to add some 300 yards to the length of the course. We went from a medium-sized project to one that involved almost every aspect of the golf course.

Course Crafters acted very quickly to accommodate the expanded project and did it consistent with their high level of expertise. The first thing they did was poison the grass on the fairways, and as soon as the grass was dead, they replaced it with new sod. In that way, the fairways would have the same grass for the first time in years.

While they poisoned the fairways, the work on the greens began. The process was a revelation to me. Prior to coring any green, about 1,500 to 2,000 GPS elevations were shot so the greens would be rebuilt in a way that defied anyone from knowing anything had been done. The next shock was when we cored the greens to the drainage system. The drainpipe that had been used after the tournament in 1958 was clay, and each section of pipe was merely butted against the next one. As we pulled the pipe out, it was evident that most of the system had never been used. If those pipes were still in use, we could have cleaned the outside and sold them! The inside was almost brand-new.

There had been tremendous progress in the design and equipment used in drainage systems since the 1950s. A new underground aeration system, which had come out of Augusta National where the Masters was played, needed to be part of our rebuilding. Sub-air systems create a way in which air can be pumped into or out of the greens as necessary to oxygenate or cool them. In extremely warm areas such as Augusta, Georgia, and Tulsa, Oklahoma, the system can include air conditioners to cool the greens. As you would imagine, Augusta has air conditioners at every green.

AN MBA THE HARD WAY

We had five greens that suffered in the heat of the summer, so they were equipped with air conditioning units to keep them healthy.

We found there was hardly any part of the irrigation and drainage system on the course that was not compromised in some way. The replacement of these and the other course repairs continued at a hectic pace. Then, once the new drainage systems were put under the greens, the rebuilding began. It was really interesting to watch the GPS elevations being used to clone the greens that had been there before. Every one would be exactly the same except for three greens. Two of those were well-known to all the golfers at the Club: the ninth and eighteenth.

Over the previous twenty years, the types of grass used on greens had caused the green speed to increase significantly. As a result, there were only two pin positions on the ninth and eighteenth that were within USGA slope specifications. We needed at least four pin positions on each green to qualify under their specs. That way, each day the USGA or PGA could move the pins to alter the challenges of the hole. We proceeded to move the ninth and eighteenth a little bit to the east of their previous positions. The front of each green was raised four inches, and the back was lowered four inches. This change gave the 2007 PGA pros at least four positions for the pins. For members' play since that time, there are even more positions, which have been well received by the membership.

The seventh hole was altered as a result of a suggestion from the golf course architect for the project,

Keith Foster. He wondered if we wanted to change the green to something more similar to what Perry Maxwell would have done. Perry was the architect of the original golf course, and Keith proceeded to give me a history lesson. After the 1958 Open, it was decided to move the seventh green away from Sixty-First Street and redesign it. By that time, Perry Maxwell had passed away, so they hired Robert Trent Jones to design the new green. I had no idea this was the case, and I don't think much of the membership knew this either. Therefore, we decided to take about 600 square feet off one area of the green and slope it in an entirely different way. We believed Perry Maxwell would have been proud of the new design.

The changes to the course were completed to allow for the course to reopen in July of 2006. As you can tell, it was a pleasure and privilege for me to have been so close to the project. It is even more satisfying as I sit here in 2011 and see what we did and how well it has worked. It was gratifying to see the aerial shots of the course during the 2007 PGA Tournament and enjoy the beauty of a single grass type covering the whole course. Today, we have John, Russ, and Keith to thank for the skill and hard work that was put into the course.

* * *

What happened next regarding Can-Oxy was gut-wrenching for everyone concerned. Still a member of the board of directors, I was very much involved. Oxy owned 30 percent of Can-Oxy, although there was little or no economic benefit to Oxy other than the dividend and the implied value of the stock if it were sold. As Ray and Dale were moving into many new ventures, there was always a need for additional capital. They decided they wanted to capitalize their interest in Can-Oxy. They actually wanted to trade their interest in the company for Can-Oxy's interest in the Yemen property.

At the time, I was also a consultant to Oxy, although no one ever consulted me. In situations such as this, it was necessary to form a committee of the independent directors of Oxy to deal with the issue from an arm's-length position. By virtue of my past experience with Oxy and my consulting arrangement, I could not be classified as being independent, even though I had been the CEO of Can-Oxy for two years and a board member for much longer. What transpired from that point on until its conclusion was totally predictable.

The relationships that had developed over the years were soon forgotten as each side tried to maximize their positions. The trade that seemed great to Oxy was ridiculous to Can-Oxy. I favored the Can-Oxy side, although no one really cared what I thought, which was no big surprise. The discussions became heated, and as best I could, I tried to act as a mediator. Dale was very upset that the Can-Oxy board did not act more gracious to Oxy during the negotiations, that they seemed to have forgotten the important part Oxy had played in Can-Oxy's success. I think I calmed him down when I said the board of Can-Oxy was doing everything he and I would have done if we had been faced with the same situation. He agreed, but he still did not like it.

The main issue was how to establish the value of the Oxy interest in Can-Oxy. The manner by which this issue was settled was nothing short of a miracle. The Ontario Teachers Fund bought half of Oxy's interest at a mutually agreed to price, and Can-Oxy bought the other half on the same terms. The deal proceeded to a closure under these terms. At this point, the name of the company could no longer be Canadian Occidental as Occidental Petroleum was no longer the majority shareholder. Therefore, a committee came up with the name Nexen, which spelled the same in either direction. They did a worldwide search to ensure no other corporation was using the name and that the word did not mean something offensive in some foreign language. So Can-Oxy became Nexen.

The Nexen board was formed without Oxy participation for the first time since 1983. Francis Saville, who was the independent chair of the board committee, called me and said they would like me to stay on the board, but I would have to sever my ties with Oxy. In other words, I would have to give up my consulting arrangement. As I thought about it, the board seat at Nexen paid four times more than the consulting contract with Oxy. However, from a loyalty point of view, I leaned toward Ray and Dale. Moreover, the principle involved, that they were asking me to compromise that relationship, irritated me.

I told Francis I would not sever my relationship with Oxy. He needed to understand: (1) my relationship with Oxy would not effect my future commitment to Nexen and (2) my relationship with Oxy was special to me and I would not compromise it. Francis came back later and said that the board agreed, and they still wanted me. I was glad I had done the right thing and everything had worked out well.

The next growth opportunity for Nexen came a few years later. As the operations in Yemen were going into the mature stage, we were trying to see where opportunity might lie. We had been aggressive from an exploration standpoint, but we had not had the level of success we needed. Fortuitously, Larry Murphy got wind of a property that Encana, a large Canadian company, was in negotiations to sell. It was a controlling interest in a field being developed in the North Sea called the Buzzard Field. The present CEO, Charlie Fischer, entered the contest with the board's approval. The property was in the stage of being developed after drilling had discovered a very large recoverable oil reserve. The state-of-the-art platforms were under construction, and production was scheduled to start in two years.

Nexen was successful in purchasing Encana's interest and, along with it, the organization that was supervising the construction phase. It was amazing to see this massive project, $2.5 billion, proceed to completion on time and within budget at a time when the price of everything was going up due to all the large capital projects going on in the world. We wondered why Encana would decide to sell a major discovery when they were so hard to find. I am sure there was a reason, but it goes beyond my ability to comprehend it. The quality of the assets purchased and the organization acquired were beyond our expectations. I thought, *Another God deal!*

To commemorate the completion and production startup of the Buzzard Field, the board took a trip to view the installation. I have been on many platforms over my career, and it was only the second time I had been on a North Sea platform (or platforms since there were three). Truthfully, there were no current platform facilities like the one at Buzzard. All of the cutting-edge technology systems you would desire are on this facility. When we toured it, there were seven wells producing at the time. Total daily production was over 200,000 BPD.

If you have never been there, I cannot explain in a way that you would understand. I had never touched the wellhead of a well producing 30,000 BPD. It was an outstanding performance by all who were involved, including the reservoir itself. It is to the credit of the management of Nexen that they were on top of an opportunity that could have passed by if they had not been alert and aggressive regarding all growth possibilities.

As I indicated earlier, I was aged out of Nexen in 2007. I was both sad and glad. I was sad that the experience with the company had ended. I had seen and been a part of so much of its history for almost a quarter of a century. I had the opportunity to run the company and be its spokesman to the public for two years. And I had great relationships with the employees and the members of the board, even though there was always some indistinct barrier between Canadians and

Americans. I discovered we don't necessarily think alike. For the life of me, I have never understood their politics and eventually quit trying. However, I was glad we lived there for a while. I especially enjoyed the *three weeks of summer*!

One of my retirement gifts was a player's jersey from the Calgary Flames, with my name and the number 24 on the back, representing the number of years I had been on the board. I am glad I do not have to travel back and forth to Canada, although the pay was good. Having traveled for more than half my life, I am very comfortable now traveling between Tulsa and Austin to see our kids and grandkids. I am mostly glad to know how Can-Oxy became Nexen and a very successful player in what is really a difficult game.

AN OLD OILMAN'S PERSPECTIVE

It was very interesting to see the initial discussion about who was responsible for the explosion and subsequent spill of oil in the Gulf of Mexico. Each of the three companies involved was pointing their finger at the other as the culprit. No one wanted to take the blame. Moreover, it is always amazing how the legal concerns rule the day that dictate: do not accept responsibility for anything. However, it does not take an MBA to determine who is responsible. Just ask, "Who pays the bills?" This is not a recent truism. It has always been that way.

Having had some experience in drilling wells both onshore and in offshore deep water, the person who pays the bills is the one who hires the contractors and service companies, develops the plan for drilling the well, supervises all the operations to see that the plan is followed, and is responsible for preventing or solving any problems that might occur. The industry refers to this company as the operator.

Also, there is no new shift of accountability that came about on the basis of new technology or philosophy of doing business. This is the way it has always been: the buck stops with the operator, which in this case was BP. To think that on a well that can cost between $100 to 200 million, the drilling contractor or a service company does anything that the operator does not know about or didn't provide for in their plans shows a complete lack of knowledge as to how the process works or at least how it should work.

The process of getting ready to drill such a well is not mundane. The plan to drill one of these wells involves the use of all information within and outside a company to complete the well within the confines of the plan and do it safely. This is especially true in the deep water Gulf; there is nothing routine. When you are operating in five to seven thousand feet of water, you must evaluate what the well is telling you in every step you take. This continuous evaluation then allows you to respond in a way that maintains control of the process under all conditions. When any sign of a potential problem is ignored, chances are that the well will respond in a way that becomes difficult to control, so you monitor the well continually and make adjustments to avoid catastrophe. The fact that this strategy works is borne out by the successful operations in the Gulf over the years.

It is not unusual in these wells that because of the conditions encountered, you lose your initial hole and have to go to what we call a sidetrack. In this case, the initial hole is plugged completely up to a new takeoff point, some 1 to 10,000 feet above the original total depth. The sidetracked hole is then drilled using a portion of the old hole. These are done with no breech of regulations and certainly no compromise of the safety of the operations. The manner by which companies arrive at their drilling plan is pretty much an industry-wide system or what we would nowadays call "best practices." I am assuming that if BP had used best practices in completing this well, there would be no problem.

I have no knowledge of the particulars of the BP well. This I do know: at least one of those messages from the well was not understood or it was ignored. I repeat that the well is always communicating to you in some way and the interpretation of those messages determines the action you take. The history of how these down-hole messages have been handled over many years, regardless of whether you are on land or in the water, provide the basis for a safe approach to a solution to any problem. It cannot be stressed how important on-site supervision by a number of people is required during specific delicate procedures, and the responsibility for that supervision can never be separated from the operator of the well, in this case BP. It is only when supervision of all the demands of drilling in potentially hostile environments is ignored that catastrophes such as the Gulf event take place.

The other thing I find hard to believe is that the CEO of the operator of the well, after a period of some sixty days, came before a congressional committee and indicated numerous times that he was not familiar with the details of what took place that led to the blowout. He had almost two months to ask all the questions necessary and to answer all the inquiries he might be asked. Furthermore, the person running an oil and gas business makes, or at least should make, monthly presentations to the board as to what is going on. As I said before, the cost of these wells are high, some as much as $300 million. The daily cost of activities can run in excess of $1 million per day. Regardless of the size of a company, they constitute a large measure of the total capital spent during the year. Also, we can see by the volume of oil that came from the well that it had huge potential and importance even to a company as large as BP. To not understand in detail what was happening on such a well on a daily basis seems nearly impossible to someone like myself, who spent a lot of his life dealing with details of similar situations.

One of the good things about Sarbanes-Oxley is that it causes boards to be very inquisitive about where large amounts of money are being spent, where high risks are involved, and the controls associated with money management. This involves the discussion of the details and techniques of drilling wells that have great potential and come at a very high cost. It is also necessary on boards in this business to have some members that can converse intelligently and with experience about the details of projects being pursued. The best way to understand risk is to have someone on the board who has dealt with the same or similar situation.

With the oil spill and considering the events of recent years, the subject of ethical conduct in business has become a hot topic. Not only do our departments of justice and treasury have concerns, but the general public has suffered tremendously because of the unethical and, in some cases, illegal dealings of a few major corporations and businesses. When things go wrong, our system looks for someone who is responsible. We then try to establish new controls that make it impossible for that situation to happen again.

What we should have learned by now is that a system of controls is not the final answer. We spent a lot of money to put controls in place through the Sarbanes-Oxley Bill (SOX), only to find out that Madoff and Sanford were not being watched. How is it that a fund of some $70 billion was not covered by the same rules that regulate corporations and businesses of all sizes, some much smaller than $70 billion?

The changes imposed by SOX were designed to minimize the possibilities of failures that affect the general pubic. Having been the chair of the audit committee at Nexen for five years when we put SOX into place, I can assure you that it did make more explicit the financial controls in publically traded companies, established accountability, and clearly indicated who was responsible. The question I can't answer, which I posed earlier, is why privately held companies weren't put under the same scrutiny as publicly traded companies. The Madoff and Sanford fiascos happened not for the lack of regulation, but for the lack of enforcement.

Of course, no matter how many laws and regulations we pass, there always will be some individuals who will find ways to slide around them for personal gain. This causes problems for the rest of us. We cannot always control other people's actions, but we certainly can control our own. Each person in business must ask themselves regularly: "To what extent do the decisions

I make in regard to shareholders' ownership, the effectiveness of the management of assets during my watch, and the way I treat and manage people reflect what I say I believe? To what degree are my beliefs evident in the way I run a company or organization?" There is no college course to help you address this issue. Each of us has to choose to make daily decisions according to what we believe is right and just. Hopefully, when we do this, we know what right and just mean.

Decisions involving people are the most difficult; decisions involving money are easier since they do not involve people directly. To be truthful, decisions that involve money seem to always involve people as well. Decisions based on less than expected performance or a breach of trust or ethics are simple. You merely point to the established standards or rules of conduct that you have set and cite the infraction. These standards and rules may be imposed by government, other organizations, or be self-imposed, but it is management's responsibility to hold themselves and others accountable.

From my years in upper management and as a Christian businessman, I have made some observations with regard to these issues. There are those who do things legally and are not ethical. They comply with the laws of the land while acting in an unfair, selfish, and greedy manner. For me, this was not an option. My code of ethics was biblical as well as legal, and what was right and wrong was decided by God, not me. The only decision I had to make was to either do things His way or another way. This sounds very simple, but it is often not easy. I would be overstating the case if I said I always did it the right way.

Again and again, both in my own experience and watching others, I have seen that it does not pay to conduct business apart from the principles in which you believe. In my case, these come from the Bible, both the Old and New Testament. Some of the truisms are:

- You reap what you sow.
- You were created to be fruitful and multiply, to be a giver not a miser.
- Treat others as you would like to be treated.
- When it comes to integrity, you can't require people around you to be something you aren't.
- A course of action to benefit yourself or your company may be legal, but it may not be the right thing to do.
- Discipline and instruct others with truth and compassion.
- If you care about those in your care, you will correct them.
- Deal with your emotions and don't let them rule your decisions.
- Forgive. Success many times follows mistakes.
- As you help others realize their dreams, you will see yours come to pass.

These are just some of the principles derived from the Bible. They are simple, make sense, and over the decades, I have seen them work.

Public schools may teach children how to read and write, and colleges may teach young adults how to earn a living, but they are woefully inadequate in teaching the governing principles of right and wrong. People who oppose teaching these principles in the schools and universities cite the fact that values and standards of behavior should be taught in the home. However, it is obvious that this education is not happening in many homes today. The large increase in single parent families, and the related economic conditions in the aftermath of what caused the situation, do not necessarily lend themselves to allowing for the necessary time for education of ethics and principles of life. Too many young people believe that what is right is what suits them at the moment. They give no thought to how their actions affect their families, their friends, their schools, their communities, or even themselves in some cases.

This is why biblical principles, which are the only principles that foster healthy relationships and sound business practices, need to be taught preferably in the home, but if not, they must be taught somewhere by someone who loves and believes in those they teach. These principles can be taught without ever mentioning the Bible or the Christian religion, by the way. You don't have to believe in God or eternal life through his Son to know what works and what doesn't work in life and in business. But I will say this: anyone who does believe in the God of the Bible knows he designed us to function a certain way in order to be successful and happy. We do not define what is right, He does. And if we live according to His design and plan, we will be blessed in every area of our lives. This does not mean that everything that happens in our lives will be without tragedy or always understood, but it does mean we can go to bed at night with clear consciences and the security of knowing the Creator of the universe has our back.

✳ ✳ ✳

It's not enough to decide what you believe and how you want your company to operate. You must communicate your vision and expectations. One of the most important factors in the success of an enterprise is communication with your employees. It is vital to company morale that they know what the leader of the company believes and how he wants them to perform both in terms of productivity and integrity. Furthermore, setting these standards does no good if the person who made them does not keep them, especially if that person is the one in charge!

It does not follow that everyone will do the right thing if they know what you expect from them. The majority probably will because they want to keep their jobs and continue to be paid. However, if you do not communicate clearly your expectations, the responsibility will be yours if they stray from or violate the principles by which you live and run your business.

In the busyness of their position, many CEOs forget that it is vital for employees to know what is expected of them operationally, ethically, and morally. What happened to Enron is a perfect example. Upper levels of management were not concerned how the business was being run by those under their oversight, probably because they were not necessarily very good examples themselves.

Business is a game, and you had better establish the rules and adhere to them because it is a game with high stakes and competition. If you play by the wrong rules, the negative effects on the people in your company may crush you both personally and professionally. Choose your focus and goals in light of your values and beliefs. When the game is about how much money you can accumulate, that objective will dominate the rules established for the game. Moreover, if a person in leadership begins to play by a different set of rules, it is amazing how quickly that style is picked up by the whole organization, good or bad. That is why it is so important for people to know what it is you believe and desire to accomplish. Then they can decide if they want to be on your team.

How do we make known to our employees what we believe, what we expect, and who we are? One of the ways that came to my mind while Cities and Oxy were going through takeovers, mergers, and extreme changes in the economic environment was to create a regular communication event that would bring everyone up-to-date as to what management knew about what was happening. I set up a monthly "Breakfast with

Dave," where anyone who wanted to could come, have breakfast on the company, and ask me anything.

It was evident after the first couple of months that there were more people eating breakfast than asking questions, so I changed the format. Questions now came to me in writing, were anonymous, and were given to someone on my staff who made a list. I had no idea where they came from. On breakfast day, I went down the list and answered all questions as best I could.

The first time we operated under this format, I was definitely under pressure. The questions were not easy for many reasons, and some did not like the answers I gave. However, they saw immediately that I would not bypass any question they asked. The great benefit was that after several months of these breakfasts, they knew me. They clearly understood my stand on all issues, the principles that guided me, and what I expected of myself as well as them. Some of the answers were not what they wanted to hear, but they knew my position.

The flip side of this, of course, was that it also gave me the opportunity to hear the thoughts and ideas of employees I might never have had the opportunity to converse with otherwise. I found that when you show people respect, you are more likely to get respect for your position, and you will always get some great ideas outside your box.

* * *

The first time I heard Henry's name was when I did business with his company, Sooner Pipe and Supply. In the early 1960s, I was responsible for up to six rigs in Odessa, Texas, each of which was drilling a new well every thirty days. I often needed supplies during the night, and the two companies I could count on for quick service were Sooner Pipe and Vinson Supply, both Tulsa companies.

After I moved to purchasing in Bartlesville in 1965, I met Henry Zarrow, who owned Sooner Pipe. I said, "Mr. Zarrow, I know you already by the quality of service I received from your company while I was in the field." I learned very quickly that his company was a true reflection of the kind of person he was and still is today.

On occasion, I have spoken to business schools on the subject of ethics and an example I use is about Henry. In the early 1980s, US Steel decided to build a rolling mill in the United States. There had not been a modern mill built to roll tubular goods in many years. It had been so long, I think they used an Italian design for the mill. There was one catch: they would not build it without commitments on the total production for three years. At the time, our industry needed more tubular goods and the commitments came fairly easily. Exxon, Mobil, and many other big company names were on board. Because of its size, Henry's company seemed out of place on such a list, but he committed for 10 percent of the plant output.

The mill was to be completed sometime in 1984. By the time the plant was completed, the need for tubular goods had gone down drastically due to a downturn in the oil business. Henry got a call from an attorney who represented one of the other companies. He explained that because of the current lack of need for tubulars, and since the same situation existed in other companies, they had found a loophole in the contract that might allow them all to get out of their commitments.

At first, Henry did not understand what the attorney was saying and asked him to repeat his position. As soon as he understood, Henry's answer was classic. "I did not read the contract and have no intention of doing so. I do know that I shook hands with the chairman of US Steel and made a commitment to him. That is my contract. I will take the pipe that I committed to take even if it causes my company to go bankrupt."

Needless to say, the person on the other end of the line did not understand Henry's thinking. What does that tell you about the ethics of the man involved? It is also true that when you put your reputation, your family's financial security, and the profits of the company you own on the line to keep your word to someone whose fortunes have reversed, you are giving faith and hope to everyone to whom you remain committed. That is an ethical lesson that will never be forgotten. It is also the reason the CEO of US Steel made a special trip to Tulsa to be present at a small gathering to celebrate Henry's eightieth birthday.

* * *

Some people forget that the United States of America came together as a result of our Founding Fathers' commitment to God. As we have progressed in time from 1776, our history reveals we have often come back to the importance of that relationship in order to survive as a nation. I believe we are entering one of those times today as our country has never been plagued as it is now with problems within our society.

I thank God I was born and still live in the United States of America: "one nation, under God, indivisible, with liberty and justice for all." The key to being unified, indivisible, free, and just, and our two centuries of becoming one of the greatest and most philanthropic nations in the history of mankind, is based on the phrase, "under God." When you are under God, you know two things: he created you for a reason, and when you meet him face-to-face, you will give account for your life. This God-perspective makes a nation great.

Recently, I challenged the author of an editorial in our newspaper who made the statement that our Founding Fathers left God out of the Constitution. I reminded him of our Founders' words from the Declaration of Independence (italics mine):

> When in the course of human events it becomes necessary for one people to dissolve the political bands which have connected them with another and to assume among the powers of the earth, the separate and equal station to which the Laws of Nature *and of Nature's God* entitle them, a decent respect to the opinions of mankind requires that they should declare the causes which impel them to the separation.
>
> We hold these truths to be self-evident, that all men are created equal, that they are endowed *by their Creator* with certain unalienable Rights, that among these are Life, Liberty and the pursuit of Happiness.

All the early writings are filled with the basis of the thoughts and action being the Bible and the God of the Bible. These are very apparent on many of the beautiful memorials in our nation's capital. George Washington asked to take his oath as our first president with his hand on his Bible. During his first inaugural address, He said,

> It would be peculiarly improper to omit, in this first official act, my fervent supplication to that Almighty Being, who rules over the universe, who presides in the council of nations, and whose providential aids can supply every human defect, that His benediction may consecrate to the liberties and happiness of the people of the United States.... No people can be bound to acknowledge and adore the invisible hand which conducts the affairs of men more than the people of the United States. Every step by which they have advanced to the character of an independent nation has been distinguished by some token of providential agency.... We ought to be no less persuaded that the propitious smiles of Heaven can never be expected on a nation that disregards the eternal rules of right and order, which Heaven itself has ordained.

The people involved in the creation of our country understood the special nature of the blessings God was bestowing on the new nation. Francis Scott Key demonstrates the special nature of that relationship in "The Star-Spangled Banner." We never sing the last verse, but here is how he penned it:

> O, thus be it ever when free men shall stand
> Between their loved home and war's desolation;
> Blest with victory and peace, may the Heaven rescued land
> Praise the Power that hath made and preserved us a nation;
> Then conquer we must, when our cause it is just;
> And this be our motto "In God is our trust"
> And the star spangled banner in triumph shall wave
> O'er the land of the free and the home of the brave!

I could go on and on citing examples, not only from our Founding Fathers, but also from the men and women who have led and fought for this nation throughout our history. It is because of these strong believers and my Christian family heritage that I had the privilege to grow up in a place of freedom: freedom to become educated, freedom to marry whom I believed was God's choice, freedom to pursue the plan and purpose he had for me, and freedom to worship him in all my endeavors.

Today, things are different. Our American values have been assaulted from every side, and being a practicing Christian is at the top of the list. I wonder if you, like myself, were offered the position of CEO of a company, and you said, "I want you to know that I will operate by the principles of the Bible to the best of my ability," would be hired or thrown out of the room? Would you be respected or despised? Would you be admired for your courage but fired for fear you would not be politically correct?

Yes, I love and thank my country for its part in the tremendous life I have been allowed to lead, but I also have lived long enough and seen enough to know that we have strayed far from being one nation under God. We must turn the ship of state back to its God-given course and purpose or my grandchildren and yours may never know some of the joys and accomplishments of life we have known. For that reason, I challenge you to do all you can to restore Judeo-Christian values to this country and the businesses and companies you run or that employ you.

Know this: many have risked their personal reputations, their jobs, and even their lives to preserve our freedom as one nation under God. To me, it is the responsibility of every American businessperson to do the same, and I hope I have and continue to do my part. We cannot fail in this! Otherwise, we will lose the creativity and true joy of owning or being a part of a business, large or small, that has the freedom to pursue new ideas, take risks, and meet the challenges of the future. Inspiration, revelation, and innovation; all these come from God. If we abandon him, we will lose our ability to be a "nation under God."

SUMMING UP MY MBA

What is it that I have learned during my career of over forty years?

1. GOD IS INTERESTED

I think the most important thing I have learned is that God is very much interested in being a part of your business life. At first, I tried to compartmentalize my life, only inviting the Lord to participate in things in which I believed He had an interest. Sometimes, I did this because I didn't want him involved, as if I could hide any part of my life from an all-knowing God! I don't know why it was that in 1970, I finally decided to let Him guide me through a career of His choice, but I am so blessed that I did.

I have stated earlier that it took some years for me to understand how He was leading me in the corporate world and how I was supposed to respond to His presence in my life. In other words, I had to discover how to live my life in light of what He had done for me through Jesus Christ and not what He might do for me in any given situation.

I always worked hard, but it became evident that I was moving much faster in Cities than I deserved based on my performance. Also, I knew that if He put me in a position, He would give me the wisdom and strength to succeed or at least do the right thing. Knowing He was behind any success I had and His support was there when things didn't go well, I kept seeking to know Him better.

I have observed that many people who advance to higher positions in the corporate world actually believe they are totally responsible for their success. I call it the "awe complex." They are in awe of their position, their power, and their wealth. They try to create an environment that acknowledges and emphasizes their importance. They often have marriage problems after they attain this position because their spouse reminds them of their humble beginnings. Many wives are left behind simply because they asked their executive husband to take out the trash after they had spent the day being admired by everyone in their "awe" environment. Their husbands "trade them in" for those who are more impressed with them and will give them the awe they believe they merit.

I was blessed because I knew my only part in the process was to respond to God's nudges, follow his wisdom, and acknowledge Him in all my ways. There were times when I would come out of meetings and ask myself, "How did I respond to those questions? I had no idea they were going to ask me about that situation!" The answer was always simple: it was a God thing. And I was always thankful!

Not every decision was prayed over and not every answer was completely obvious. Business moves faster than that. In most cases, I made decisions as they were required and dissected them afterward. In business, we spend a lot of time in a post-audit of the projects and areas on which our success is dependent. Personally, after I made a full commitment to the One responsible for where I was, I tried to do a post-audit of my personal decisions to make certain they reflected who I said I was. There was always time after work, when I couldn't sleep or when I was traveling, to analyze my decisions. Not once did I ever conclude that God had not been interested in every detail of my business life.

2. PEOPLE ARE MORE IMPORTANT THAN THINGS

It was much easier to deal with the issues of things than people, but the issues of people are more important. Surrounding myself with people who would challenge me to be better than I was, and maintaining good relationships with everyone I could, has been a key to success in all my endeavors. I have learned to let God help me, and I also have learned to let others help me as well. As an American "pull-yourself-up-by-your-bootstraps" male, allowing other people to assist me required me to grow in the grace of God!

Clydella has always been my greatest help. She says that all I had to do after we moved was walk into a new office and tell my new assistant how I liked my coffee. She, on the other hand, had moved into a new house, in a new city, had to put the kids into new schools, and locate grocery stores, doctors, and dentists. Then there was the question, "Where do I find a friend?" She became an expert at doing all those things, although she never thought she would have to use that expertise so often in the course of my career.

What she may not realize is how deeply grateful I am to her for being a willing partner in life and doing all God required of her so beautifully. She has taught me and demonstrated to me what I have always believed: we should never sell ourselves short as to what we are capable of accomplishing in our lives. God built into each of us the potential to be anything we desire to be if we work hard and trust Him for the rest. We are born to be more than we can ever imagine. Clydella exemplifies this to me, and she continues to encourage and inspire me.

I wish all my career relationships were on the same level as my personal relationships. For many reasons already stated, when you are making hard decisions that greatly impact your organization, close relationships are difficult. When you never know what changes you might have to make in personnel, you tend to avoid becoming close to anyone to ensure your own personal protection. As a result, most people at the top of organizations do not have close friends within the organization. Good, bad, or indifferent, that's just the way it is. I am thankful that Dale and I remain good friends even after years of working together.

With regard to relationships in general, we hear this said a lot these days: "It's not about you!" But the question we must ask then is "Who is it about?" If it's not about me and it's not about you, then it is probably about someone much greater and more important than all of us. I can say with total certainty that that someone is Jesus Christ. It has been, is, and always will be about Him in my life. This understanding and my relationship with Him bring the proper perspective to every relationship I have. He inspires me to love and care for my wife, my family, my friends, and my neighbors as He would love and care for them and as I have experienced His love and care for me.

As a result of this perspective, I have enjoyed and continue to enjoy tremendous relationships in my personal life. Some of these relationships made a crucial difference to me personally as well as to the companies I served, and some of these relationships continue to bless me today. Most of these people will be my brothers and sisters throughout eternity, and that is the greatest joy of all. In the end, even death cannot separate us.

3. THE BIBLE HAS THE ANSWERS

If my successes are due to my relationship with Jesus Christ, then most of my failures were based on the statement: it's all about me! This is because the basis for all sin is self-centeredness. We want what we want, when we want it. Clydella and I look at the world our grandkids are traversing and see that self-gratification drives most everything, from movies to advertising to video games. Even some of the lessons taught in the public schools encourage self-centeredness.

I have seen how self-centeredness is behind every crime, and in the business world, self-centeredness has caused corporate leaders to be more concerned about the bottom line than the people who owned the companies they served, the welfare of their employees, or even the legal and ethical ramifications of their decisions. Government suffers the same issues. Regulation has helped, but it cannot provide the ultimate answers because people must interpret and enforce them.

What I am leading up to is that as long as there are flawed humans on the planet, there will be problems. Things will not be perfect. Original sin exists just as sure as gravity exists, and Jesus is the answer to original sin; however, even after being saved, we are still tempted and sometimes fall. In a devotional titled *Perhaps Today*, Tim LeHaye and Jerry Jenkins wrote, "Becoming a Christian can never cancel our fallen nature. Nor will it exempt us from seducing temptations." I thank God I received Jesus as my Lord and Savior as a child, and I am glad I will go to heaven when I die. But in the meantime, I need help to combat my tendency to be self-centered. That's where the Bible comes in. This amazing book holds the answers to the all the questions I ask in my daily life. There is no other book like it, and that is one of the reasons it is the best-selling book of all time.

Some people say the Bible is too rigid, and it does not apply to today's world. All they have to do is watch the news and read the prophecies in the Old and New Testaments to see what a false assumption that is! Early on, I was intrigued with Bible prophecy. Many things that were prophesied in the Old Testament have taken place and are recorded in our history books. These events happened just as foretold, down to the details. The most powerful example, of course, is the conception, birth, life, death, and resurrection of Jesus of Nazareth. He fulfilled every prophecy regarding the Messiah who would redeem mankind, so I have little doubt He will complete the job in the future!

In more contemporary times, I was a teenager when we saw the formation of the State of Israel in 1948. It happened just as the Bible predicted: in one day! One vote of the United Nations reestablished the nation and homeland for the Jewish people, something that had never occurred in history, and Israel remains because of many miracles that have taken place since. William Albright, a Semitic language professor at Johns Hopkins, said, "No other phenomenon in history is quite so extraordinary as the unique event represented by the restoration of Israel. At no other time in history, so far as it is known, has a people been destroyed, then come back after a lapse in time and reestablished itself. It is utterly out of the question to seek a parallel for the recurrence of Israel's restoration after 2,500 years of former history."

After traveling to so many countries for business and some also for leisure, our trip to the Holy Land in 1990 was by far the most memorable. Walking where Jesus and His disciples walked was almost overwhelming, and the day we crossed the Allenby Bridge linking Jordan and Israel was the day Iraq invaded Kuwait, obviously something we will never forget. Israel is probably the only place we would go back to visit because of what it has always represented. There, the Bible is not just alive in your heart but everywhere you go.

If I want to know what's going to happen in future world events, I only have to read my Bible.

But prophecy is not the only way God speaks to me through his Word. There is a verse in the book of Hebrews, chapter 4 and verse 12, that says God's Word shines on my life and reveals what is right and what is wrong, what is God's way and what is self-gratification. In other words, reading my Bible keeps me straight, on the right path, and not compromising my faith or witness of Jesus Christ. Any book that can do that is highly relevant to any time in which we live!

As you have read through this book, you have seen the situations I have been in and the decisions I have had to make during the course of my career. You might ask, "What gave you the sense to do the right thing over and over again, even when it might have adverse consequences?" Just pick up a Bible and start reading! The same principles that inspired me to try and stay on the right path will do the same for you.

4. YOU ARE BLESSED TO BE A BLESSING

There is a core set of biblical values that I have tried to adhere to in my Christian life, God-given principles that are his plan for living a great life. However, that doesn't mean I haven't changed my mind about a few other things. As I have gotten older and as I have experienced and grown in understanding, I have altered my assessment of some things and of some people.

A good example is my initial remarks about Boone Pickens. I did not agree with some of his business practices, but what I learned from what began with his purchase of Cities stock in 1981 was immeasurable. It taught me about the inevitability of change, the speed by which it can occur, and how God would be there to help me through it. In that sense, what Boone did was a special lesson to all in this business. Would I have rather learned this lesson another way or in class? You bet your life! But today, I respect Boone Pickens because of his tremendous commitment to Oklahoma State University. His gifts to that institution have changed the future for all who would attend for generations to come. I have seen pretty big companies whose annual capital budgets were less than what he has donated in total to OSU! He could have spent all of his money on himself, but he has not done that. He has given so that others can succeed.

Tulsa is a community noted for its philanthropists, and I have been fortunate to know and learn from some of the finest. One of the most successful businessmen in the city is George Kaiser. He is not only one of the smartest men I have known, but he is also one of the most generous. Another couple I have looked up to through the years is Henry Zarrow, who I wrote about earlier, and his wife Anne. Their example of compassionate hearts for giving has set an example for all of us to follow. Anne died a few years back, but Henry carries on what he and Anne started. Of all the men I have known, Henry has influenced me more than anyone in both my business and personal life.

One year, Henry called and asked if I had an SUV. I said yes. He asked if I would go with him to Walmart the next day. The weather was about to turn very cold, and when I picked him up, he explained that we were going to buy clothes for the Day Center for the Homeless. When we checked out at the register, we had seven carts overflowing with socks, underwear, insulated and otherwise, stocking caps, gloves, sweatshirts, and so on. We had actually destroyed whole aisles of clothes. We probably also ruined their computerized inventory system, which is based on usage.

Henry wasn't finished. We then went to Sam's to buy shirts and pants and everything else that was needed. By the time we finished, the only available space we had remaining in the SUV was where we sat. We took the clothes to the old Day Center facility, and that was the first of a yearly excursion with Henry. In recent years, as Henry has been unable to participate, Clydella and I have become Henry in disguise. It has become part of our Thanksgiving and Christmas season. It also must be noted that the facility we now deliver to is a state-of-the-art building Henry and Anne were catalysts to see built some years ago. It all came about when Anne saw a baby sleeping on the cold floor of the old building and told Henry she was going to do something about that. And she did!

Knowing people like Boone, George, Anne, and Henry and many others in the Tulsa community teaches us that God didn't bless us just to bless ourselves, our families, and our own concerns. He blessed us to bless those who cannot help themselves and to help those who want to improve their lives and the lives of their families. You may say, "Well, I don't make a lot of money. It's all I can do to pay my bills." Then I would still encourage you to give whatever you can give: your time, your care, your talent, and whatever finances you are able to give. Again, this is another biblical principle: you will reap what you sow, and you cannot imagine the rewards of giving until you begin to do it.

5. NO MATTER WHAT HAPPENS, GOD IS THERE

Clydella knows more than anyone does what difficulties we faced, and sacrifices we made as a family, so that I could walk the professional road God had for me. It was hard for me to miss so much of my children's growing up years, but having the wife I had made all the difference, and we also had three outstanding and understanding children. Scott and his wife Erin have given us two wonderful granddaughters, Emily and Lindsey. Stuart and his wife Cathy have also given us two very special granddaughters, Annie and Ella. Our two sons and their families are inspirations to us. They know more about their children than I ever knew about them. As I have said before, God was smiling when he gave us four granddaughters after raising three boys! We are privileged to spend a lot of time with these very special girls.

Our middle son Steve and his wife Debbie passed away over two years ago. Their story was not a happy one. We tried as best we could to help them deal with their problems, but we were not successful. Sometimes, the impact of bad choices cannot be turned around, and it does not follow that if we have given our lives to

Jesus, we won't make bad choices in life. The memories of their good times remain with us, however, and we have the great hope of seeing them in heaven.

The death of a child is one of the hardest things you can experience in life, but God was with us and continues to hold us together and comfort us in the valleys of life. We are so blessed that he is always there.

I have no idea what the rest of our life will be about. The future, just as our life to this date has been, is in the hands of a Father who is much wiser than anyone.

God has used and continues to use many amazing people to be my teachers, mentors, and guides as I walk out my MBA degree. The degree will never show up in my earthly resume, but it is in my heavenly one. While it took longer to obtain, it is probably much more demanding and much more fun.

In securing a college MBA, you spend a lot of time dealing with case studies; my experiences were the case study. In college, you deal with a lot of hypothetical situations, examining various solutions and assessing the potential impact of all decisions. Little was hypothetical on the road to my MBA. I would encounter a situation and deal with it as quickly as conditions demanded. I learned from it afterward.

The great thing is that many of the events during this process were fun: the sale of CITGO to Southland, the acquisition of Wascana and Elk Hills, the discoveries in South America and Yemen, and the opportunity to participate with incredibly knowledgeable and effective people.

I have enjoyed writing these memories, but my career and my life are special for only one reason: there is a Creator who has unlimited humor to put someone like myself in a position that could only have a successful outcome with him as my guide. Praise God!

ENDNOTES

1. When pipelines are laid, it is done on right-of-ways that are secured through the purchase of land. Those lanes of land have to be mowed and maintained so that, in the event of leaks, they can be seen by people walking the line or viewing them from the air.

2. Fee land includes both the surface and mineral rights of the land. Obviously, this would appeal to Sam!

3. Plays are formations in the earth that produce oil.

4. A block is usually 5,000 acres of territory (land or sea) that the states put up for bid for drilling rights.

5. A trend is where there is a concentration of oil and gas.

6. Seismic shooting is a process whereby vibrations are sent into the earth to bounce off underground rock formations and determine the possibility of oil and gas reservoirs.